I0094171

INDIGENOUS KNOWLEDGE SYSTEMS AND INTELLECTUAL PROPERTY IN THE TWENTY-FIRST CENTURY

Perspectives from Southern Africa

Edited by

Isaac N. Mazonde & Pradip Thomas

Council for the Development of Social Science Research in Africa

University of Botswana

World Association for Christian Communication

In association with the University of Botswana
& the World Association for Christian Communication

ISBN: 2-86978-194-6
ISBN 13: 978-2-86978-194-8

Typeset by Daouda Thiam
Cover image designed by Ibrahima Fofana
Printed in Senegal by Imprimerie Graphiplus, Dakar, Senegal

Distributed in Africa by CODESRIA
Distributed elsewhere by African Books Collective, Oxford,
Web site: www.africanbookscollective.com

The Council for the Development of Social Science Research in Africa (CODESRIA) is an independent organisation whose principal objectives are facilitating research, promoting research-based publishing and creating multiple forums geared towards the exchange of views and information among African researchers. It challenges the fragmentation of research through the creation of thematic research networks that cut across linguistic and regional boundaries.

CODESRIA publishes a quarterly journal, *Africa Development,* the longest standing Africa-based social science journal; *Afrika Zamani,* a journal of history; the *African Sociological Review; African Journal of International Affairs* (AJIA); *Africa Review of Books; Identity, Culture and Politics: An Afro-Asian Dialogue* and the *Journal of Higher Education in Africa.* It copublishes the *Africa Media Review.* Research results and other activities of the institution are disseminated through 'Working Papers', 'Monograph Series', 'CODESRIA Book Series', and the *CODESRIA Bulletin.*

CODESRIA would like to express its gratitude to the Swedish International Development Cooperation Agency (SIDA/SAREC), the International Development Research Centre (IDRC), Ford Foundation, MacArthur Foundation, Carnegie Corporation, the Norwegian Ministry of Foreign Affairs, the Danish Agency for International Development (DANIDA), the French Ministry of Cooperation, the United Nations Development Programme (UNDP), the Netherlands Ministry of Foreign Affairs, Rockefeller Foundation, FINIDA, NORAD, CIDA, IIEP/ADEA, OECD, IFS, OXFAM, UN/UNICEF and the Government of Senegal for supporting its research, training and publication programmes.

Contents

Contributors

John Kiggundu is currently a Professor in the Department of Law, University of Botswana. He studied Law at Makerere University and obtained his Doctorate in Law in 1985 from Queen Mary and Westfield College, University of London. Between 1985 and 1988, he taught law at South Bank University, London. Professor Kiggundu specializes in Company Law; Intellectual Property; Mercantile Law; and Private International Law. He has published extensively in learned international journals and other publications in the areas of Company Law; Intellectual Property; Mercantile Law; and Private International Law. He is the author of *Company and Partnership Law in Botswana* (2000); *Mercantile Law in Botswana: Cases and Materials* (1998); *Private International Law in Botswana: Cases and Materials* (2002); *How to Study Law in Botswana* (2004); *Botswana Company Law Service* (2005); and he is the co-author of *A Guide to Intellectual Property Law in Botswana* (2001).

Mogomme Alpheus Masoga (Phd) was at the time of contributing to this book, employed by the National Research Foundation (NRF), Pretoria, South Africa.

Kgomotso Moahi is a lecturer in Library and Information Studies at the University of Botswana. She teaches in the areas of health information systems and information science in general. Her research interests are in health information systems, indigenous knowledge systems and intellectual property rights. She also has an interest in information systems in general, and in particular in how such systems can be brought to bear on development. Kgomotso Moahi holds a PhD in Library and Information Studies, and is currently heading the Department of Library and Information Studies.

Isaac Mazonde is an Associate Professor of Human Geography in the University of Botswana, where he has worked since 1978 when he joined as a

Staff Development Fellow in the former National Institute of Development Research and Documentation. His research interests include social organization for economic production, minority groups, technology transfer, food security, and since 2001, he is now focusing on research in research management. He has published extensively in all these areas, and is Director of Research and Development, University of Botswana.

Siamisang Morolong is a lawyer by training and is currently a lecturer, in the Law Department, University of Botswana. She has taught the subjects of Property Law Intellectual Property Law, Business Law and Environmental Law at the University of Botswana. She has researched and published in the field of Intellectual Property Rights and is member of the Botswana National Technical Committee on Intellectual Property Rights.

Mogege Mosimege (PhD) is an ethnomathematician who has researched and published extensively in ethnomathematics and mathematics education in general, and also in indigenous knowledge system. He has been actively involved in IKS debates and was part of the team that developed the IKS Policy in South Africa. He is currently a manager of the Bilateral Relations Unit in the Department of Science and Technology in South Africa.

Otsile Ntsoane (PhD) is Deputy Director, Department of Science and Technology, Pretoria, South Africa. He has researched widely on technology transfer issues relating to indigenous knowledge systems and he continues to publish in this field, where he is also used extensively by the South African government to present especially on adaptations of new indigenous technologies.

Francis B. Nyamnjoh is Associate Professor and Head of Publications and Dissemination with the Council for the Development of Social Science Research in Africa (CODESRIA). He has taught sociology, anthropology and communication studies at universities in Cameroon, Botswana and South Africa, and has researched and written extensively on Cameroon and Botswana, where he was awarded the "Senior Arts Researcher of the Year" prize for 2003. His most recent books include *Negotiating an Anglophone Identity* (Brill, 2003), *Rights and the Politics of Recognition in Africa* (Zed Books, 2004), *Africa's Media, Democracy and the Politics of Belonging* (Zed Books, 2005), *Insiders and Outsiders: Citizenship and Xenophobia in Contemporary Southern Africa* (CODESRIA/ ZED Books, 2006).

Wapula Nelly Raditloaneng (Phd) is a multidisciplinary Sociologist of Development trained in Health Education, community water supply and sanitation and Adult education. Her area of specialisation in Adult Education includes research methods, curriculum development and writing course modules for open and distance education, poverty, social context, gender issues and Adult Basic Education. She has accumulated a wealth of experience from different workplaces as a Rural Sociologist. Currently, she is a Lecturer in Adult Education, University of Botswana.

Alinah K. Segobye Archaeology Unit, Department of History, University of Botswana.

Associate Professor **Pradip Thomas** is at the School of Journalism & Communication, University of Queensland. He has published widely on issues related to intellectual property and communication rights. His latest (2006) publications include the jointly edited volume (with Jan Servaes) *Intellectual Property Rights and Communications in Asia: Conflicting Traditions,* Sage, and the article 'Communications Rights in the Information Society (CRIS) Campaign: Applying Social Movement Theories to an Analysis of Global Media Reform' in the *International Communication Gazette.*

Introduction

Isaac N. Mazonde

The subject of Intellectual Property Rights (IPRs) and the related theme of indigenous knowledge systems have moved to the centre of academic discourse within the context of innovation and the commercialisation of knowledge. Specifically, wealth is no longer reckoned in terms of physical assets alone. In fact, in the knowledge economy that characterises the twenty-first century, intellectual property, or the product of the mind, have become more important than physical wealth in the form of buildings and other physical assets.

But again the developing world lags behind in taking advantage of the move towards the commercialising intellectual property. The traditional imbalance between the North and the South, which has for long manifested itself mainly through trade, is replicated even in tapping intellectual property given to residents of the developing world remain largely unable to define their intellectual property rights. Again, the West exploits Africa and the rest of the developing world by expropriating indigenous knowledge systems and patenting them in the West.

This imbalance formed the overarching reason for the workshop supported by the London-based international NGO, the World Association for Christian Communication (WACC). The workshop, held from 26 to 28 November 2003, at the University of Botswana, was aimed at offering academics and artists an opportunity to discuss intellectual property rights, laws and practices, and their implications for cultural creativity in Africa. It focussed on many issues, including copyright matters and how these affect Southern Africans and their work. Issues discussed also included the responses by African writers and artists to the increasing privatisation and commodification of creativity and cultural production by corporate business. The discussions were based on the different assumptions people held or still hold about ownership and control of knowledge, ideas and creativity underpinning different attitudes to the copyright debate. Special focus was rightly given to the Indigenous Knowledge Systems (IKS) regime and how it is affected by the apparent approaches involving the commercialisation of community knowledge and outputs. A major outcome of the workshop was to raise awareness of the complexities of Intellectual Property Rights (IPR) in IKS contexts and to get artists, scholars and others, to think about how they can stop the IP exploitation they are subjected to by the West.

The papers included in this volume present a snapshot of IKS issues in the Southern, thereby providing the reader with a broad perspective of the problem, as well as providing a wider array of suggestions on the way to combat it. For example, some papers present the problems that are inherent in attempting to formulate intellectual property legislation over communally held resources in the public domain where plants with potential commercial value exist. Other papers focus upon equally indivisible properties such as traditional music that is associated with a tribe and not an individual. The point here is that the West has succeeded in patenting these aspects of the African heritage, and has then claimed intellectual property rights over them, at the expense of the owners of these assets.

While Information Technology (IT) has greatly enhanced communication across the world, and has made a clear contribution to development and the quality of human life, it has impacted rather negatively on copyright issues. The use of the Internet has resulted in copyright being infringed upon. This subject is taken up at some length in this volume. Fortunately, a way out of the problem has also been proposed.

What makes the volume invaluable is the way problems are raised and then solutions proposed. This approach makes this volume a major resource for scholars, practitioners and others working in the areas of intellectual property rights and indigenous knowledge systems.

Although the papers that appear in this volume generally indicate that southern Africa is still way behind in terms of putting in place a structure for harnessing intellectual property for its people and environment, the workshop itself had an impact on national legislation in Botswana. As a consequence of this workshop, the Botswana government has used the material to produce a chapter on indigenous knowledge in its revised intellectual property legislation that was enacted in 2005. This is indicative of the fact that this book forms a watershed in southern Africa' initiatives towards commercialising intellectual property, and especially in creating a firm and viable basis for driving locally-based innovation that has a potential for expanding the region's economy.

Finally, I must recognise the role played by Professor Francis Nyamnjoh, who initiated the workshop, and wrote the concept paper that Successfully became the basis for WACC support for this workshop. that is the basis of this book.

1

Contesting Space and Time: Intellectual Property Rights and Indigenous Knowledge Systems Research - A Challenge

Mogomme Alpheus Masoga

Introduction

I enter into debate on Intellectual Property Rights and Indigenous Knowledge from the standpoint of both Indigenous Knowledge Systems (IKS) and African divination perspectives. 'Culture', according to the New Partnership for Africa's Development (NEPAD) document is:

> an integral part of development efforts on the continent. Consequently, it is essential to protect and effectively utilize indigenous knowledge that represents a major dimension of the continent's culture, and to share this knowledge for the benefit of humankind. The New Partnership for Africa's Development will give special attention to the protection and nurturing of indigenous knowledge, which includes tradition-based literacy, artistic and scientific works, inventions, scientific discoveries, designs, marks, names and symbols, undisclosed information and all other tradition-based innovations and creations resulting from intellectual activity in industrial, scientific, literary or artistic fields. The term also includes genetic resources and associated knowledge (Clause 143, p.48).

Further, according to the document, NEPAD's leaders:

> will take urgent steps to ensure that indigenous knowledge in Africa is protected through appropriate legislation. They will also promote its protection at the international level, by working closely with the World Intellectual Property Organization (WIPO) (Clause 144, p.48).

Conversations on indigenous epistemologies have become a centre of debate in and outside Africa. NEPAD was not mistaken in embracing IKS in the agenda to develop Africa. IKS refers to knowledge and technologies around communities indigenous to a particular space and context. The understanding of IKS should include both spiritual and material aspects, as well as the complex relation between them. The effort to engage IKS partly tries to understand and explore the potential contribution to local development and its protection and use for the benefit of its owners where it is practised (NRF/ IKS Focus Area brochure, 2002). For the purpose of this presentation, the word 'culture' is strategically replaced by IKS to be in line with NEPAD's formulations.

The interest to further IKS research and it promotion was firstly taken up seriously in South Africa by the Council for Scientific and Industrial Research (CSIR), involving a number of tertiary institutions. The CSIR attempt was kick-started in 1998 and strengthened by the new research support structure namely, the National Research Foundation (NRF) - a combination and reconfiguring of the Centre for Science Development (CSD) and the Foundation for Research Development (FRD). The NRF looked at a number of research foci: included in them was the promotion and research on indigenous epistemologies. The programme to support and promote research in IKS was started in the first quarter of 2000. The establishment of the IKS Focus Area was made possible by the allocation of a ring-fenced amount of R10 million by the Department of Arts, Culture, Science and Technology (DACST) to the NRF. The programme provides funding for research undertaken by individuals and teams at tertiary institutions, science councils (SCs) and other research-based organisations, non-governmental organisations (NGOs) and communities in South Africa. Under the new funding framework it operates as the IKS Focus Area. The IKS Focus Area has six sub-themes or sub-focus areas namely:

(a) The nature of Indigenous Knowledge (IK), Indigenous Knowledge Systems (IKS) and Indigenous Technology (IT);
(b) Traditional medicine and health;
(c) Indigenous food systems;
(d) Socio-cultural systems;
(e) Arts, crafts and materials; and

(f) Cross-cutting and supportive issues in IK, IKS and IT.

According to the NRF's stance on IKS, it is maintained that:

> We have to understand Indigenous Knowledge (IK) and its role in community life form an integrated perspective and include both spiritual and material aspects, as well as the complex relation between them. At the same time, it is necessary to understand and explore the potential contribution of IK to local development. The protection of IK and its use for the benefit of its owners and the communities where it is practised, require research. Research into IKS, however, should ideally be carried out with the participation of the communities in which it originates and is held. (www.nrf.ac.za/funding/guide/iks.stm).

In response, Seepe (*Tribune Magazine*, 2001: 52) partly concluded:

> The exclusion of blacks in research can be linked to issues of epistemology, and the political and cultural location in which the research process takes place. We err if we consider the research debate within the social sciences and humanities as simply an issue of skills, techniques and procedure.

Further, in this regard, Le Grange (2001:139) strongly argues that:

> What is referred to here is a concern about epistemological justice in that disparate epistemologies have not been equally adopted in or compared equitably within participatory action research process. This is an important concern because Western epistemologies continue to dominant 'other' ways of knowing.

The above asseverations indicate the fact that the West has to begin to recognise the African space when conversing with her. Western dominant knowledge is no longer the sole epistemology when dealing with developing countries. It is important thus, for the West to converse with Africa acknowledging their capacity and space in their (African countries') knowledge systems in technology, biological resources and natural resources production (Ntsoane 2000: 43).

It is the opinion of the present author that for any genuine conversation to take place between the West and Africa, the matter of space has to be looked into in a serious light. It is a fact that the current IKS debates in and outside Africa displays a lack of space. The indigenous epistemological space is invaded and occupied apparently without any ethical considerations.

One wonders whether there is any regard for ethics and philosophical consideration in this boundary 'jumping'. It is within this context of contestation that this paper is presented to look critically at the IKS and African and Western discourses of culture for the development of Africa. The author aims to make use of his personal experience in engaging and disengaging this discourse of power regarding IKS research.

Broadening the horizons

Mbiti (1970) asserts that culture is a phenomenological concept through which people retain their self identity, build their views, and symbolically express a shared historical experience, and thereby create a sense of collective cultural identity. It follows that culture is embedded in the life of the society with its variety of aspects such as material culture, painting, drama, philosophy, etc. On the whole, culture helps people to affirm their comprehensive well being in the world around them. Again culture is contained in what people are capable of doing and retained as a source of building confidence in themselves and in relation to others. African culture will always continue to pose questions about 'unusual happenings'. This is so despite encroachment by modernisation and globalisation. Culture will always under-gird every reasoning that encounters humanity. For example, imagine a young well-qualified engineer driving from Sandton (one of the suburbs in Johannesburg, South Africa) in her new car and a top-of-the-range laptop computer on the seat next to her, to see her grandmother and ask her to bless her new property. She drives to Giyani KaMalamule (a dusty and remote village in Limpopo Province, northern South Africa). On her arrival, a diviner-healer of the clan meets her and immediately sprinkles substances on her car. The *ngaka* (diviner-healer) then gets a goat slaughtered for this special occasion. Vakokwani (grandmothers) of the entire clan sing praises to the young lady. For some, this may be strange. For African people, it is a daily occurrence. It is central to their lives, philosophies and cultures. Modern life does not exclude this particular part of African spirituality. The ancestors are not outdated, nor out of touch with current developments and the challenges and demands of modern living. They are a living part of life - they know about laptops and new cars.

After the second White Paper on International Development, the Commission on Intellectual Property Rights (CIPR) was set up to look at how the global rules and practices on intellectual property rights might better serve the interests of poor people and developing countries. This overall aim is better encapsulated in the message from the British Secretary of State for International Development, Clare Short (2001, www.iprcommission.org/index.asp) that:

> We believe that a basic framework of intellectual property (IP) law is important in developing countries in order to attract foreign investment and modern technology. It is also necessary to encourage research to provide drugs for the diseases of poverty and to make possible tiered

pricing. But the key question that needs to be addressed is whether the world's IP arrangements help or hurt poor people.

In 1982, the World Intellectual Property Organisation (WIPO) in collaboration with the United Nations Educational Scientific and Cultural Organisation (UNESCO) through a Working Group agreed that:

- Adequate legal protection of folk-knowledge was desirable;

- Such legal protection could be promoted at the national level by model provisions for legislation;

- Such model provisions should be elaborated so as to be applicable both in countries where existing legislation could be further developed;

- The said model provisions should also allow for protection by means of copyright and neighbouring rights where such forms of protection could apply; and

- The model's provisions for national laws should pave the way for sub-regional, regional and international protection of folk-knowledge (WIPO/GRTKF/IC/2/8).

This recognition of IKS is reflected in the launch of all, recently (15-16 December 2001), the present author attended the launch of the National Centre for Traditional Healing and Reconciliation at Vlakplaas, Pretoria in South Africa. The launch was both directed and facilitated by the Indigenous Knowledge Systems Secretariat. One of the prime aims of this project is to create, encourage and support IKS Small, Micro, and Medium Enterprises (SMMEs).

The above-mentioned local and international efforts are noted. However, it becomes imperative to mention at this stage that what pervades all these attempts (and many others) is the dominant language of economics. All mention the fact that all IKS attempts should be economically viable in order to sustain poor communities. The other closely connected concept in this context is the language used, which claims to conceptualise this economic viability or sustenance. The language belongs to the centre-space and 'speaks for' the margin-space. In this regard, it is the centre that speaks 'on behalf of' and claims to take into cognisance potencies that exist in the margin-space. One can demonstrate this better by citing one proposal that was sent to the NRF for funding of an IKS collaborative project between the University of the North, South Africa and the University of Natal (Pietermaritzburg, South Africa). In this proposal, the hypothesis states that:

> This study is that African belief systems demonstrate the nature and usefulness of certain medicinal plants and animals. The assumption is that many of these beliefs are embedded and therefore unsaid. It is the

task of the research to uncover them and demonstrate their significance. The study is based on the further assumption that the medicinal plants themselves are merely surface indicators of deeper socio-cultural realities. As signifiers they are gateways through which researchers may access these realities and try to understand their social significance (Joint Proposal submitted to the NRF by A Balcomb, M.A. Masoga, S.T. Kgatla and L. Ngoetjana, 3 July 2001).

The above-stated hypothesis indicates that the research respondents will be tuned to speak for the research study. This clearly indicates how power directs and misdirects at times. The present author was directly involved in the above-mentioned collaborative research project. He became aware, having consulted with his research interlocutors, of the power dynamics involved in this research process. The following are some of the excerpts taken from a two-hour interview that the author had with *Ngaka* (Sepedi for diviner-healer) Maamushi, one of the diviner-healers in the Limpopo Province (dated 23 October 2001, translated from Sepedi into English). The interview focussed on the NRF collaborative research project indicated earlier on.

Masoga: 'What do you think about the subject of beliefs, and their social implications for medicinal plants?'

Maamushi: 'There is a problem with the use of the concept: medicinal plants as well as 'belief systems' behind medicinal plants. The idea of medicinal intervention (*mekgwa ya go thusha motho*) should rather be used instead of medicinal plants' conceptualisation. This is because there is a wide variety of plants that could be used for specific interventions. The intervention is important, not the plant. Similarly the term 'belief system' should be replaced by the term 'social reality' (*seo bophelo e leng sona*). You young researchers suffer from the Western way of looking at things. You come to us with words and expect us to give you the African equations of them. That is simply wrong! You have got to change the manner in which you conduct your research. African belief systems must have a holistic approach. Plants cannot be viewed in isolation from the spirit world. They are also connected with the animal world - both domestic and wild. All are part of an environment that is composed of the forces of air, water, fire and earth! Healing in such a world is always physical, psychological, spiritual and social!

The above points to a number of significant areas in terms of IKS research and the debates. Firstly, the research respondents have their own space that they do not wish invaded without following the prescribed protocol. This margin-space is considered by its occupiers to be central in their life and philosophy. Secondly, the margin-space of these respondents has its specialised language that should be learned in order for one to begin to understand it. Thirdly, one is strongly cautioned not to be too much of a reductionist. James Cox's views on methodological conversation make sense. He maintains that:

> We can understand those who are different from ourselves with confessionally endorsing their world views. Yet, we do affirm methodologically what they affirm thereby experiencing what they experience (1966:166).

This explanation or perspective clarifies confessional conversion as opposed to methodological conversion. As Cox (1996:168) maintains, 'Confessional conversion surreptitiously moves the study of religion away from science into theology'.

In this case, methodological conversion allows one to suspend the rules of autonomous rationality and abide by the rules of religious faith while at the same time playing by the rules of scientific rationality (Cox 1996:168). Cox uses the term dia-topical hermeneutics as opposed to an interpolation approach.

Obviously, attempts to protect and promote IKS end up exposing who 'real ab-users' are, i.e. those who are concerned about the protection of IKS. This translates into a power game and invasion of the space that is occupied by the 'powerless'. One cannot avoid noticing the variables: centre-space and margin-space. It is the opinion of the present author that most debates between the West and Africa are trapped in the centre-space and its specialised operations.

In this context, one area of struggle is to overcome the obvious gap between the periphery (margin-space) and the centre (centre-space). One would be tempted to propose that there should be a partnership between centre and periphery that ultimately goes beyond the two dichotomies. The challenge remains: is it possible for the centre to move to the periphery? The concern calls for 'genuine' conversation between the centre-space and the margin-space. This concern notes power as both concept and practice in the whole process. Glossing over it would not resolve the endemic condition. Grappling with and acknowledging its serious implications, offers one the opportunity to devise new and innovative strategies in dealing with it.

A Case for the Conversational Approach

This paper proposes the conversational approach (qualitative research of ethnographic nature) in addressing the asymmetry propensity that exists between the centre-space and margin-space. IK research should offer both the centre and periphery a space to converse and converge. No IK or IPR is adequate unless it wrestles with the question of power relations. The idea of forging an interface (Serote: 1998) between the centre and periphery does not at all help or come to any solution of the problem we are all facing. It is necessary for displaced discourses to occupy their space and converse with centralised discourses. The jargon dialogue as indicated elsewhere (Grenier: 1998) will suffice. The conversational research model should be considered as one of the options in narrowing the gap that exists between the two discourses (margin-space and centre space). This will hopefully handle discursive borderlines and open up a possibility for the many institutions of conversation.

Conversation allows openness, presence, honesty, life, honest critique and tapestry. In this process, the opportunity arises for 'trained' researchers to gain deeper insight of the realities of the margin-space discourse. The margin-space occupiers bring popular critique into the centre scholarship. Their discourse addresses and impacts on countless life issues. In the process, issues raised are problematisations which under-gird the lives of common people and are absent from institutionalised published institutions. The centre-space capitalises on systems from which only they themselves or a few others benefit. The margin-space is all about life and opens one to the reality or face-to-face presence and contact. The voices echoed in it present one with a mirror of life and presence. There is no place for multiplicity of absences, or its empty promises and elusiveness. This, definitely, offers the centre-space an opportunity to be immersed in the conversation of presence and contact: real presence and real contact.

The margin-space produces and masters its own research context dispositions. It is communal and co-operative in essence. It connects the disconnected, and opens up stifled channels of energy. It is communal and cooperative in essence. It clears up blocked conversations and jumps and deconstructs existing boundaries, and ultimately re-ordering these channels and boundaries linking and connecting them for the purpose of advancing the dignity and integrity of all involved. Open and honest critique is guaranteed in the margin-space. Margin-space discourse seeks the bravery of the significant, the oppressed, and the silenced, but also reports failure. In this case, the discourse takes place in public and not in terms of conceptualised ritualised and intellectualised discourse that incarcerated and silenced the prophetic and life-giving voice. If listened to closely, within its given space, it is definitely not intimidated by any type of power.

Conclusion

This paper has raised a voice that might disturb those coming for the first time into the world of IKS research. It should firstly be noted that questions and issues raised should become issues and questions of contention for doing IK research and IPR. The relatively good researchers are those who 'agonise' in their attempts to collect and contribute 'new' - if there is such a thing as 'new' ideas - and information to the corpus of knowledge. Second, researchers in the field of IKS should be reminded to tread carefully in the area of epistemology. They have to form a 'rapport' of 'trust' in engaging 'local research participants' - because it is the latter's space; they own and direct it. Who can claim their space? Surely, only they themselves! They have the ability to direct their margin space to the centre. As Ntsoane (2000:43) rightly points out,

> Building on the indigenous knowledge of rural communities is the route to take when dealing with developmental projects. It is only when Western countries begin to respect the IK of developing countries and acknowledge that the people of the countries including Botswana and South Africa have knowledge systems that are unique and appropriate to their socio-economic sustainability that a dependency on Western countries and their exploitation of Africa's natural resources for the benefit of capitalists will be challenged.

References

Battiste, M., and Henderson, J. Y., 2000, *Protecting Indigenous Knowledge and Heritage: A Global Challenge*, Saskatoon, Purich Publishing Ltd.

Brush, M., and Stanbinsky, D., 1996, *Valuing Local Knowledge: Indigenous Peoples and Intellectual Property Rights*, Washington DC, Island Press.

Cox, J. L., 1996, *Methodological Considerations Relevant to Understanding African Indigenous Religions in Africa*. United Kingdom, Cambridge (Roots and Branches).

Grenier, L., 1998, *Working with Indigenous Knowledge: A Guide for Researchers*, Ottawa, IDRC.

Le Grange, L., 2001, 'Challenges for participatory action research and indigenous knowledge in Africa', *Acta Academica*, vol. 33, no. 3, pp.136-150.

Mbiti, J. S., 1970, *African Religions and Philosophy*, London, Heinemann.

Ntsoane, O., 2000, The Implications of Intellectual Property Rights on Indigenous Knowledge Systems in Southern Africa, Unpublished MA Dissertation submitted at the University of the North West.

Posey, D., 1996, *Beyond Intellectual Property: Towards Traditional Resources Rights for Indigenous Peoples and Local Communities*, Ottawa, IDRC.

Scott, P., 1997, 'Changes in knowledge production and dissemination in the context of globalisation', in Cloete et al., eds., pp.3-12.

Serote, W., 1998, 'One Fundamental Threshold', World Intellectual Property Organization, Roundable on Intellectual Property and Indigenous Peoples.

2

Intellectual Property Challenges in Africa: Indigenous Knowledge Systems and the Fate of Connected Worlds

Pradip Thomas and Francis B. Nyamnjoh

The commoditisation of intangibles has been a characteristic feature of globalisation in the twenty-first century. In an age characterised by the 'knowledge economy' and the ever-deepening embrace of the market, intellectual property has been invested with economic value greater than the value given to tangible property. In the knowledge economy, value is assigned to intangibles, to any exchangeable content available in digital form. In this sense the knowledge economy's raw material 'information' is very different from the raw materials that fuelled previous economic epochs related to agriculture, industry and manufacturing. Digitized information as knowledge, as product and process, as input and as resource has become a jealously guarded, prize commodity – and the value of such commodities has cumulatively increased in the context of the many marriages that have taken place between previously separate technologies and in the context of the globalisation of the digital. However, the globalisation of this model of growth has by no means led to the total displacement of earlier traditions of production – for instance the agricultural economy that remains the only basis for subsistence and survival for many millions of people around the world. The current attempts to enclose all available knowledge within a singular IP tradition are problematic for more than one reason. There are communities around the world who have always had a different relationship to knowledge from the dominant norm. Their knowledge has been critical to their physical, cultural and onto-logical survival. At the same time there are many traditions of knowledge that are rooted in a nation and that to some extent form the basis for national and cultural identities. These traditions of knowledge that are expressed through culture, heritage, tradition are now located, in the context of IP, within the category 'Indigenous Knowledge Systems' (IKS).

While a number of scholars have written on various aspects of the cultural politics and political economy of copyright – Lawrence Lessig (2001, 2004), James Boyle (1996, 1997), Rosemary Coombes (1998), Ronald Bettig (1996), Siva Vaidyanathan (2001), Michael Brown (2003) among others – IP issues are no closer to being resolved and are bound to remain contentious for some time, given the intrinsic nature of the digital to defy any attempt at its enclosure. Matters are not made any easy by the fact that companies like Sony and Philips for instance make profits selling DVD burners while also taking lead roles in industry lobbies committed to enforcing the copyright writ. A recent example of a copyright controversy is the attempt by the music industry to stymie peer to peer file sharing of the Sydney-based PtoP network, Kazaa. While the copyright industries have launched a major international publicity initiative to educate the public on the wrongs of piracy and have spared little effort assisting numerous countries in the developing world to establish enforcement agencies and tighten up penalties for copyright infringement, there has been little or no media exposure to the strategies used by the music industry to lobby for the extension of copyright or for that matter on the many ways in which the music industry uses copyright to make profits from a variety of formats – from ring tones to CDs. In late September 2002, five of the world's biggest music companies – Universal, BMG, EMI, Warner Music and Sony along with three retail chains in the USA – agreed to pay US$143 million as a settlement for the charge of price-fixing brought by attorneys representing forty-three states in the USA. It has been decided that US$63 million from this amount will be used to compensate consumers who overpaid. The companies involved have also been directed to distribute 5.5 million CDs to schools and non-profit organisations. Remember, these are the very companies currently exploring encrypted and copy-protected CDs that will play on a home stereo but not in a CD-ROM drive. Who says that piracy is the only problem faced by the music industry?

At the Heart of IPR are Competing Philosophies of Ownership and Control

There is legitimate concern about the growing privatisation and commoditisation of knowledge production and consumption engineered and sustained by global corporate capital. As the market takes on a global embrace, cultural communities and creativity diversity at individual and collective levels are increasingly prey to the logic of privatisation and commoditisation that is in a sense a key characteristic of consumer capitalism. Communitarian and humanistic traditions of cultural production and consumption are often marginalised in this process.

All over the world, even sectors previously at the margins of the profit motive, such as indigenous cultural forms – music, weaves, symbols, artefacts, knowledge of natural resources, dance steps, motifs – are steadily becoming privatised and have become part of the circuits of knowledge production, distribution and consumption. A consequence of such commercialisation and privatisation of social and spiritual resources, it could be argued, is their debasement and trivialisation, which in turn purges them of most of the symbolic capital relevant to the cultural communities. Often, the indigenous communities who have been dispossessed of their knowledge are never compensated even as they are denied control of their own traditions and identities (Brown 2003: 5). By using their power over global economics, corporate business asserts formidable control over global creativity, imposing yardsticks of thinkability, do-ability and desirability determined exclusively by market considerations. Consumption replaces culture as the ultimate measure of civilisation, and resources are invested in the trivialisation of human creativity in favour of standardised, routinised, and streamlined production that promotes uncritical consumption, which in turn blunts creativity. The same considerations make it possible for capital to comb the globe like a giant compressor dispossessing whole communities and individuals of their creativity and patrimony. The tendency is clearly to reduce all ownership to individual ownership, and to deprive community and collective ownership informed by philosophies of personhood and agency that treat individuals and groups as interconnected and interdependent (Brown 2003; Rowlands 2004).

In spite of the fact that two-thirds of the world live within another matrix of development, governed by other technologies, frameworks, options, hopes, expectations, the logic of information is nevertheless pervasive and global. As markets penetrate into the deepest rural hinterlands, and as information becomes an essential raw material in all major processes and commodities, from the manufacture of genetically modified food (GM) to retroviral drugs for AIDS, to surveillance, knowledge is steadily being displaced from the hitherto protected, narrow boundaries and confines of the clan, tribe, village, community and is being redesigned and reconfigured in response to the asking and dictate of global capital. Culture too has become fair game in the business of commoditisation. The tourist industry, the market in cultural artefacts and the global fashion and leisure markets have also played their part in accentuating legal and illegal trade in culture. This process of displacement, in spite of increased understandings of the worth of traditional knowledge, is currently not being monitored to the extent that it ought to be. In fact in contrast to the many international efforts to protect the products of the copyright industries from pirates, and the many transnational efforts to globalise enforcement, the lack-lustre policing of bio-prospecting is nothing short of scandalous. While open borders are notoriously difficult to police, bio-prospecting is not of recent provenance but has been part of the strategy of multinational industry for many decades. The provision of bi-lateral aid has also been used as the means for channelling 'essential' knowledge back to donor countries. While a few of the larger countries in the developing world have begun to create their own databases – for instance the National Bureau of Plant Genetic Resources in India – the very fact that USAID has contributed to forty percent of the costs of setting it up 'in return for which American scientists have access to seed and data for research' (1992:8), and the fact that companies like Hoechst (Germany) which owned 86,000 patents in 1995 had already screened 90,000 soil samples from India (1996:151), indicates the extent to which aid and bio-prospecting have reinforced the terms of neo-imperial conquest. If this is the reality in a relatively 'strong' developing country, countries in the South have probably fared a lot worse.

If this tendency is anything to go by, the future is one where collective ownership and control of the world's resources and creative diversity is likely to be appropriated by a few individuals who may personally not be creative but who are certainly rich enough to dispossess communities trapped in poverty. The enactment of supportive intellectual property legislation has certainly protected the interests of global capitalism. The information economy is founded on enclosures around knowledge and information.

IP and the Digital Economy: A Fait Accompli

While globalisation has occurred at a variety of levels, the global expansion of trade in knowledge, and the economic value given to knowledge as a tradable commodity, have led to the strengthening of intellectual property regimes at a variety of levels – global, regional, national – and to the globalisation of the IP writ. The global significance of IPR needs to be seen against the foreground of accelerated multilateral and bi-lateral trade negotiations at a variety of fora – WTO, NAFTA, MERCOSUR, APEC, ASEAN, EU – along with numerous bi-lateral negotiations that are committed to the expansion of the market and in particular the information economy. Along with the informationalisation of the productive sector there has also been an 'informationalisation of life processes' leading to what one critic has described as the 'homologisation of information', to equivalences between human biological information and non-biological information. In other words genetic information as much as the codes used to guide 'smart' bombs, operate on the Windows platform and the latest Hollywood blockbuster share a common language – the language of the digital. 'Enclosures' that are being built around this extraordinarily textured, global, weave of digital information have become a rich vein of pickings for all manner of knowledge czars – from private sector companies such as IBM and Monsanto to state-run institutions including the security and military apparatuses.

Why and how did this mode of information become so universal and dominant within a relatively short space of time? To a large extent, this had to do with economics, the imperatives of trade and the politics of comparative advantage. The global recession in the 1970s and 1980s, the fall in the price of primary commodities and the decline in manufacturing exposed weaknesses in the traditional economy that was based on industrial manufacturing. There was a need for alternative means of value creation. By the early 1980s, computing had emerged as a powerful tool in value creation. The products and processes of digital capitalism were projected as a potential means of reinforcing global economic dominance by the USA, Western Europe and Japan over the rest of the world. There was a need to extend, maintain and reinforce market share in the trade of new informational products and lay down the terms of protection for trade in the emerging digital economy. Proposals related to Trade Related Intellectual Property (TRIPs) were included in the Draft Final Act submitted on 20 December 1991 at the Uruguay round of Multilateral Trade negotiations of the General Agreement on Tariffs and Trade (GATT). This proposal was opposed by the developing world, Brazil and India in particular, who were of the opinion that the UN-related, World Intellectual Property Organisation (WIPO) that had been set up to deal precisely with IP issues, ought to oversee global IP-related concerns. Vandana Shiva (1998:85), a foremost critic of the proprietary economy, has observed that TRIPs was not a result of democratic negotiation. Rather, it was an imposition by three organisations, '... the Intellectual Property Committee (IPC), Keidanren, and the Union of Industrial and Employees Confederation (UNICE)'. Shiva points out that 'IPC is a coalition of 12 major US corporations: Bristol Myers, Du Pont, General Electric, General Motors, Hewlett Packard, IBM, Johnson & Johnson, Merck, Monsanto, Pfizer, Rockwell and Warner. Keidanren is a federation of economic organisations in Japan, and UNICE is recognised as the official spokesperson for European business and industry'. It is interesting to observe that among the twelve US corporations behind the IPC initiative are key corporations that are contemporary leaders in the new synergistic industries – the life sciences, the cultural industries, computing, and military technologies.

The Trade Related Aspects of Intellectual Property Rights (TRIPs) regime's accent on the global harmonisation of IP legislation leaves little room for manoeuvre for countries involved in trade negotiations under the aegis of the World Trade Organisation. All countries including the least developed countries that have been granted limited handicaps are expected, in return for this granting of a 'grace period', progressively to liberalise their economies, and to harmonise their internal IP legislation with global requirements. Developing countries are faced with, as Mansell and Wehn (1998: 206) have pointed out, four choices in the light of the emerging IP regime – '... the choices are to increase the level of monitoring and enforcement to avoid the risk of increased liability, to insure against the risk of liability, to accept the risk and hope to escape legal liability, or to transfer the liability risk to another party'.

Industry has continued to play an extremely critical role in the framing of global IP futures. This has led to radical revisions to the meaning of IP. Copyright, historically speaking, was an agreement between the creative artist and the state. This contract ensured that the state, in exchange for the temporary protection of, and reward for creative endeavour (provided the copyright owner kept his or her mouth shut on matters related to State and Faith), returned this creative expression to the public domain after a fixed period. To reiterate, copyright was conceived as a social contract – between the rights of the creator of a work and the public domain – in which the immediate, short-term grant of monopoly rights and the protection of the moral and monetary interests of the creator, was balanced out against the long-term patrimony of the public domain. This core balance that ensured private-public trade offs has been steadily lost. Creative artists no longer own what they have created. Their rights are transferable, in hock to those that have the money power to introduce their work to the marketplace. Today the benefits of copyright are enjoyed for the most part by owners of IP that invariably are the cultural industries, rather than those who created the work either as individuals or through team effort.

The 'African Native' as an Object of Research

Not only does the current IP regime championed by global capitalism privilege individual over collective ownership, it is informed by an idea of legitimacy predicated upon hierarchies of knowledge, creativity, valued and humanity that, in the case of Africa, date back to the beginnings of unequal encounters with Europe. Such hierarchies have since the slave trade and colonial times facilitated collusion between science and ideology, placing the power of definition firmly in the hands of the western (or western-trained) expert who, drawing on dominant western world views and systems of social organisation, has enjoyed studying down and studying out of competition the creative differences of the world. Intellectual property produced in such a situation of hierarchies and unequal power relations is highly problematic, especially when copyrighted.

Thus our argument that, given the reality of unequal encounters and the hierarchies that characterise individuals and communities, copyright regimes ought to be a lot more thorough, investigative, negotiating and nuanced in the way copyright is attributed. Let us consider the case of Africa where many excesses have been committed against whole communities in the name of scholarship. How proper would it be in the results of research pregnant with glaring prejudice and racism were to be copyrighted and made available for public use, despite its obvious falsehood and opportunism? Should the publications and public lectures of anthropologists be copyrighted, if these consist of belittling photographs of the so-called 'primitive natives' and are written with scant regard for the dignity and humanity of those they have studied down? Some might argue as often they do, that the photographs were taken with the consent of the subjects in question. But just how informed was that consent? Most villagers and slum-dwellers in Africa who are photo- graphed, for example, are quite unaware of the fact that the photograph, which an apparently friendly 'anthropologist'

> (or whatever researcher) has asked to take of them, is going to serve as slides in public lectures, dessert at anthropological meals, or the cover picture of a copyrighted book in a strange, distant country, where they might never go. Some of the most exploited in this regard have been the San, Basarwa or the Bushmen of Southern Africa, the Pygmies of Central Africa, and the Masai of Kenya. It is commonplace in Europe and North America to find 'attractive glossy photographs and films of Bushmen dressed in fur and leather, and ornamented with glass bead and ostrich shell necklaces, hunting with bow and arrow, living in close symbiosis with nature, and generally being their gentle, cheerful and authentic self in a harsh and arid environment. Sometimes it is dead Bushmen who are stuffed and displayed in museums and other public places (as "intellectual property"), as was the case of the famous El Negro of Spain, before his reluctant repatriation and reburial in Botswana' (Parsons 2002).

It is doubtful if the Bushmen would necessarily see these pictures and displays as attractive or as celebrating their culture and symbiosis with nature. And so one may ask, were villagers as informed about the world as their anthropologist researchers, would they have allowed their photographs to be taken if they had known of the representational politics of the visual im- agery? And in this regard, are not certain anthropologists taking undue ad- vantage of the people they study, to proceed to copyright 'intellectual prop- erty' that is clearly contentious, and in certain cases, not the fruit of their 'individual' or 'original' creativity imagination, despite what they may claim?

Were African village communities to take stock of what has been published and copyrighted on them in the name of social science, they are most likely to lampoon researchers and refuse further cooperation in any future social scientific research. We are not unaware of the 'racist Afrikaner Volkekunde (apartheid ethnology) ... which treated Africans as archaeological specimens', as it fed apartheid with conceptual rhetoric to justify the marginalisation and distortion of African cultures through bantustanisation. The fact that such unethical research provided apartheid with the arguments it needed to minimise the empowerment that Africans and their communities could draw from their cultures to fight domination, did not disqualify it against being copyrighted. One of the consequences of such research and its translation into apartheid policies, was the space constraints they imposed on black people, forcing them 'to "shrink" to fit the limited space they found themselves in', to a point where it is not going to be easy for them 'to stand up and walk tall' or to free themselves from the mind set of calling a bed home, as Ramphele puts it. Examples abound of copyrighted research work by pro-apartheid scholars, which tended to glorify whites and debase blacks as it sought to justify racism. The consequence was reduction in self-esteem and self-confidence among blacks, and the over-glorification and exaggerated self-importance among whites and the narrow focus of intellectual property rights that the world views of which they partake have engineered.

Such copyrighted but problematic research does not seem to have diminished with the end of apartheid, as the following example shows. South Africa is currently involved in a land restitution process, whereby people who have in the past been removed from land are claiming their land back. This case is about a strategic piece of land at a border area called Nmampo [pseudonym], close to the Kruger National Park. Before this land was declared a buffer zone to be occupied by the South African Defence Force under apartheid, it used to belong to a Manata community [pseudonym] who had their own chief. These people were forcibly removed and settled across the tarred road. The piece of land was fenced and the people were never allowed in, not even for the purpose of performing their rituals, even though their kin are buried there. After 1994 there was no need for this buffer zone any more, so the former owners of this land lodged a complaint to the Land Restitution Commission, requesting restitution.

According to Ananu [pseudonym], a white professor at the University of Manata [pseudonym] was commissioned by a ministry to look at how best the piece of land, coveted both by the Kruger National Park and the village community previously dispossessed by the apartheid government, could be utilised. Here is an excerpt of his account:

As part of the project, the professor was expected to visit the concerned villagers and find out exactly what they had in mind about using the land once it was returned to them. However, given the anger that these villagers and their chiefs had over whites (mostly academics) for the role they played during apartheid, it was unthinkable that this white fellow would be able to carry out a research of this nature. All that the professor did was to use his black undergraduate students. He selected native Manata students to get involved in this research. Everyday he picked these students and drove them to this area, which is about 60–80km from the university. On his arrival to the area, he would drop them by the corner, which was just a kilometre from the villages. These students would go in and get information as if it was for meeting requirements for their own degrees. On realising that they were Manata, the villagers were happy to cooperate with the students. The villagers never saw the professor, nor did they ever know what really the information was about. Had they known, they would have been very cautious, since there was (is) already a committee, representative of all villages, dealing with this crisis.

On completion of the research, the professor wrote a report, which he sent to the ministry, recommending that the land be turned into a 'Reserve' which would be part of the Kruger National Park. On hearing the news the villagers were surprised since they never knew of such project conducted in order to know how their land could be best utilised. All they knew of were students who came to ask them questions. Fortunately enough, one of the villagers knew one of the students. The villager reported this to the committee. The student was traced and brought to the gathering of villagers. It was this student who revealed all of this (Ananu [pseudonym], personal communications).

This account is not only an example of covert research, but also a case of manipulation and endangering of students by a professor. It also raises the question of the ethics of a researcher tendering for a study, which he/she could not personally carry out, but intellectual property over which he/she ultimately claims through copyrights. How else can outsiders justify that they qualify to study the social reality of others, except, of course, by claiming a value-free status for social science, and arguing that being predicament-oriented is a recipe for ideology, not objectivity?

Those who copyright social scientific research in the form of books, journal articles, documentaries, and so on, would be less eager to grant copyright with had they greater consciousness of the enormous power social scientists wield because of their knowledge and responsibility in determining the conditions of research. Power which enables social scientists to manipulate those they study drawn from relatively powerless and poorer segments of society who are often without the freedom to assert their rights and avoid exploitation. Should not there be a series of test questions to establish the extent to which a researcher has been ethnical, for his or her work to be considered for copyright? Questions based on the following considerations:

–Are you as a social scientist aware that your research practices could jeopardise the health, attitudes and personalities of those whom you research, exposing them to unwanted embarrassment?

- Determine the extent to which the research seeking copyrighting unnecessarily harms those who are studied, does so against their will, and out of proportion to the scientific and practical benefits due from the study;
- Seek to know the extent to which the social scientist's research respects the privacy and anonymity of those studied;

These issues are significant ones, as the history of the social sciences is littered with examples of researchers who have taken undue advantage of the protection afforded them by academic ivory towers from the outside worlds they study. Journal editors and publishers should penalise researchers for unethical conduct, refuse to confirm intellectual property right over research reports of studies if those researched have been unnecessarily harmed or experimented upon without their consent. If scholars are dishonest enough not to admit that cut-throat competition for scientific stardom often leads them into dishonest practices (forged or fabricated data, falsified or invented results, plagiarism, piracy, hoaxes, etc.), what chances are there that they will forsake copyright in the public interest?

The publication and copyrighting of research findings poses serious ethical problems. Often the researcher benefits, for example, by publishing the information furnished by those he or she has researched. But what do the individuals and communities get back in return? How often do researchers consider a restitution visit back to the community or people they studied, to share with them their findings as well as find out what the community makes of their conclusions? How many have bothered to share their royalties? How many would stand or even consider the idea that research ought to be something more participatory, with the research individuals and communities actively involved in determining not only what should be researched, but how and by whom such research should be done? To make matters worse, most research reports are published in and copyrighted by scholarly journals that are quite inaccessible in language and location to the ordinary people. Novels, films, radio and television documentaries, photographs, short stories, and epics could be alternative ways of feeding the data obtained back into the community studied. But few researchers or their institutions would accept such modes as scientific enough for academic titles. Few would even contemplate including members of studied communities on defence committees or juries. Yet it is important that the researched individuals or communities be given the opportunity to feed back into the findings and conclusions of those who studied them, and consequently share the copyright. Parallels exist between the way researchers appropriate the otherwise collective work of their field situations and studies, and the tendency by big business to appropriate the world's individual and collective creativity through a narrow IP regime that clearly privileges profits over people, and the individual over the collective.

The Marginalisation of IKS

Calls are growing for the commoditisation trend to be contained, tempered or resisted, such that human creativity can continue to serve the best interest of humanity, which is only possible through cultural production and reproduction that brings the greatest good to the greatest number. As Brown (2003: ix) notes, hardly a month passes today 'without a conference examining the ethical and economic questions raised by the worldwide circulation of indigenous art, music, and biological knowledge', which, prior to the late 1980s was hardly an issue. As Brown rightly argues, while it does not make sense for ethnic communities to define their cultural practices as property that cannot be studied, imitated, or modified without permission by outsiders, nor is it possible for democratic states to provide absolute cultural protection to indigenous peoples without contradicting the rights of the general public, it certainly makes sense to strike a healthy balance between the interests of indigenous groups and the requirements of liberal democracy, by aiming for a philosophy of cultural ownership that recognises and represents individual and collective rights, commercial and public interests (Brown 2003: 7-9).

To harness the greed of insensitivity or, in Brown's words, 'the dangers of totalising solutions to complex social issues' (Brown 2003: 8) in favour of need, would necessarily entail a regime of ownership and control that seeks conviviality between individual and collective interests, and appeals to a more negotiated understanding of intellectual property rights – one that marries individual rights and community rights, without making a dictator of the one over the other. As is the case in Africa and elsewhere, in many communities at the margins of capitalism, the knowledge of oral cultures that is not recorded in any tangible material form is deemed to be in the public domain and therefore is 'appropriatable'. The knowledge economy however 'does not recognise the fact that culture-based mediation of knowledge in traditional societies continues to be germinal expressions of community, an aspect of living traditions'. In other words, current neo-liberal and corporate insensitivities to other regimes of ownership and control that have tended to over-emphasise individual creativity over collective production, must be challenged with abundant evidence drawn from marginalised cultures and world views on the different philosophies that have inspired social organisations based on negotiated claims of rights and entitlements over time. Such alternatives have sought to empower the individual but not to the detriment of the community, and to reward personal creativity without denying or seeking to appropriate for personal profit the collective creative efforts of particular communities and cultures.

Strengthening the IP Writ

We are living in an era characterised by an unprecedented assault on the intellectual and global commons – common resources, shared traditions, cultural practices, ways of life – all these are being invested with monetary value and judged according to their dollar value rather than by their social worth. New traditions of practice that have the potential to contribute to the making of another world, for example the hardware and software of new networked technologies are also fast succumbing to myriad forms of licensing arrangements and to restrictive patents and copyright contracts that will ensure knowledge monopolies in perpetuity. This is unfortunate, not least because new technologies and new possibilities for networking – for instance the original vision of the Internet (Version 1) was based on a knowledge embrace for the many rather than for the few. The extensive terrain covered by the Trade Related Aspects of Intellectual Property Rights (TRIPS) treaty, the binding nature of this agreement, the global harmonisation of IP law and the emergence of a raft of new laws with the potential to contribute to global standards – the World Intellectual Property Organisation's (WIPO) Copyright Act (1996) and the US Government' Digital Millennium Copyright Act (DMCA) (2000) – point to the direction that the world is heading towards – a world characterised by a knowledge imperium, knowledge available only for a fee.

Whereas a number of 'moral' issues have been raised by antagonistic movements such as the free software movement, creative licensing schemes and copyleft, there are few if any contemporary media or culture-based scholars who have consistently explored IP in the context of the indigenous knowledge systems with the same amount of rigour. This has resulted in a situation where IKS related explorations are carried out by indigenous groups themselves, individual scholars, by NGOs, by government agencies and by intergovernmental organisations. There are few internationally recognised spokespersons for IKS with the exceptions of David Posey, Kamal Puri, Vandana Shiva – and the lack of a critical mass. There is little consistency in lobbying efforts – despite the fact that the concerns have led to the framing of The Mataatua Declaration on Cultural and Intellectual Property Rights of Indigenous People (1993) at the First International Conference on the Cultural & Intellectual property Rights of Indigenous People, Whakatana, Aotearoa, 12–18 June 1993 and the establishment in late 2000 of the WIPO Intergovernmental Committee on Intellectual Property and Genetic Resources, Traditional Knowledge and Folklore. Some governments, as for instance those of China, India, Thailand, Peru and Costa Rica, have established their own sui generis IP laws that acknowledge the specificity of IKS, although it is anybody's guess as to whether such legislation will have primacy in a court of law over the more dominant, globally applicable IP conventions and treaties. It is this crisis of global legitimacy that is threatening to marginalise IKS to second cousin status. It would seem that unless the developing world in particular makes a strong and determined stance on the validity of IKS as a human right and the basis for cultural survival, there is little hope of IKS becoming a globally recognised right. Botswana's protection of the Hoodia cactus as much as India's protection of the Neem – while remaining of great symbolic and cultural importance, is bound to remain a fringe item, destined for home consumption – if it does not figure in a global movement, supported by the media and other interests, committed to creating a global awareness of IKS as integral to cultural survival and as the right to remain human. At the same time, it would be absolutely critical that the complexity and systemic integrity of IKS is preserved and not compartmentalised into discrete parts as per the requirements of the modern IP system. Contemporary expressions of the communication rights movement while cognisant of the more 'sexy' contestations related to IPR have little to say of IKS. While the communication rights movement is currently committed to a smorgasbord of issues that it simply does not have the resources to deal with, and may, in hindsight, not be the most appropriate platform to deal with IKS, it certainly makes sense for an independent transnational grassroots movement or one that is related to existing networks that have a definite commitment to IKS such as the Third World Network, ETC, and ActionAid to campaign for the full recognition of IKS on a par with dominant IP systems.

References

Bettig, R., 1996, *Copyrighting Culture: The Political Economy of Intellectual Property*, Colorado/Oxford. Westview Press.

Boyle, J., 1996, *Shamans, Software and Spleens: Law and the Construction of the Information Society*, Cambridge, MA.; London, England, Harvard University Press,.

Boyle, R., 1997, 'A Politics of Intellectual Property: Environmentalism for the Net?' (pp.1-23), http://www.wcl.american.edu/pub/faculty.

Brown, M.F., 2003, *Who Owns Native Culture?*, Cambridge, MA., Harvard University Press.

Coombe, R., 1998, *The Cultural Life of Intellectual Properties: Authorship, Appropriation, and the Law*, Durham/London, Duke University Press.

Lessig, L., 2001, *The Future of Ideas: The Fate of the Commons in a Connected World*, New York, Random House.

Lessig, L, 2004, *Free Culture: How Big Media Uses Technology and the Law to Lock down Culture and Control Creativity*, New York, Penguin Press.

Mansell, R., and When, U., 1998, *Knowledge Societies: Information Technology for Sustainable Development*, Oxford, Oxford University Press.

Mooney, P. R., 1996, 'The Parts of Life: Agricultural Biodiversity, Indigenous Knowledge, and the Role of the Third System', *Development Dialogue*, 1-2.

New Scientist, 1992, 'Is India selling its seed bank short?', *New Scientist*, Vol, 135, Issue 1838, 12 September, p. 8.

Parsons, N., ed., 2002, 'Introduction: El Negro and the Hottentot Venus: Issues of Repatriation', (Special Issue) *Pula: Botswana Journal of African Studies*, pp.3-7.

Rowlands, M., 2004, 'Cultural rights and wrongs: Uses of the concept of property', in K. Verderey and C. Humphrey, eds., *Property in Question: Value Transformations in the Global Economy*, Oxford, Berg, pp. 302-319.

Shiva, V., 1998, *Biopiracy: The Plunder of Nature and Knowledge*, Totnes/London, Green Books/Gaia Foundation.

UNESCO, 'The Mataatua Declaration on Cultural and Intellectual Property Rights of Indigenous Peoples', Available at: http://www.iprlawindia.org/iprlaw/ resourcedetail.asp?ID=301&channellid=&DType=4

Vaidhyanathan, S., 2001, *Copyrights and Copywrongs: The Rise of Intellectual Property and How it Threatens Creativity*, New York and London, New York University Press.

3

Intellectual Property Law and the Protection of Indigenous Knowledge

John Kiggundu

Introduction

Intellectual property law rewards and protects the fruits of intellectual endeavour.[1] The subject covers patents, industrial designs, trade marks, utility models, copyright and neighbouring rights, and confidential information.[2] The general aim of intellectual property therefore, is to protect the ownership of creative ideas, such as inventions, designs and works of art and literature. The law protects such intellectual property by giving the registered owner of an invention or piece of work the right to stop others from copying and/ or selling it.[3] In this paper, the term 'indigenous knowledge' is used to refer to the intellectual endeavours of indigenous individuals and communities in developing countries in general, and Botswana in particular. The term therefore covers indigenous works of art, music, literature, medicine and manufacturing processes. 'Indigenous knowledge' is also referred to as 'folklore' and in this paper the two terms will be used interchangeably. The forms of expression of folklore are: folk tales, folk poetry and riddles; folk songs and instrumental music; folk dances, plays and artistic forms of rituals; and drawings, paintings, carvings, sculptures, pottery, terracotta, jewellery, basket weaving, needlework, textiles, carpets, costumes, musical instruments and architectural forms. This paper is an examination of how intellectual property law attempts to protect indigenous knowledge.

Identification of the Problem

Intellectual property law as we know it today was developed entirely by developed countries in order to reflect and enhance their cultural advancement and preserve their values. Copyright was developed to protect the literary and artistic works in Britain, Italy, France, Germany and other countries. Patent law and the law of designs were developed to protect the inventions of the Industrial Revolution and other technical developments. Trademark law was developed to protect symbols of national and international trade such as names and logos. At a very early stage in the development of these laws, the developed countries realised the need for co-operation and harmonisation. They therefore entered into international treaties on the various aspects of intellectual property. These treaties are: the Paris Convention on Industrial Property 1883 and the Berne Convention for the Protection of Literary and Artistic Works 1886. It can be seen that indigenous knowledge of the developing countries did not feature at all in the genesis of intellectual property law. When the colonial powers such as Britain, France, Italy and Germany colonised the developing countries, they transplanted their Intellectual Property law to these countries with the sole intention of protecting the intellectual property that they brought with them to facilitate exploitation, and any intellectual property that their nationals might develop while in the colonies. This colonial intellectual property law did not reflect the culture and values of the indigenous communities. Such intellectual property is known as dependent intellectual property. Protection in the colonised country depended on protection in the colonising country. In the case of Botswana for example, this dependent intellectual property remained in place until 1996. Before that year, intellectual property was governed by the Copyright Act,[4] the Patents and Designs Act,[5] the Trade Marks Act,[6] and the United Kingdom Trade Marks Act.[7] The relevant statutes on patents, trade marks and designs did not permit any person to register a patent, trade mark or design unless the patent trade mark or design had first been registered in the United Kingdom or South Africa. A further disadvantage of the legislation was that the owner of a patent, registered design or trade mark would, if he wished to sue in Botswana in respect of an infringement, have to do so under the terms and conditions of the legislation in place in the United Kingdom or South Africa, whichever would be applicable.[8] The enactment of the Industrial Property Act in 1996 marked the advent of independent intellectual property legislation in Botswana. Some developing countries still have dependent intellectual property legislation while others have gradually eliminated it since the attainment of independence.

During the colonial era, the colonial powers plundered indigenous knowledge in their colonies and repatriated as much of it as they could back to the developed countries. They repatriated artefacts, paintings, mummies, jewellery, ancient literature and historical documents, plants, animals and entire manufacturing processes. Famous examples of indigenous knowledge repatriated to the developed countries include: the Elgin marbles taken by the British from Greece and still in the British Museum; an original Ethiopian Bible taken from Ethiopia and recently returned to the University there; an Egyptian bust of Nepotete taken to Germany after excavation and now in a German Museum; an Egyptian mummy of King Rameses I which was taken to America 140 years ago and kept at Emory University which has just returned it to Egypt; El Negro taken from Botswana and whose bust was only returned to Botswana recently; and Saartjie Bartman taken from South Africa and whose body had also just been returned to South Africa for burial. One can only lament at the revenue lost which would have been obtained by the countries involved if these treasures had been left and preserved at home.

The Interface between Intellectual Property Law and Indigenous Knowledge

The issue here is whether intellectual property law at both national and international level can effectively protect indigenous knowledge.

A. Confidential Information

One of the best ways of protecting intellectual property and indigenous knowledge is by keeping it confidential. If the owner of intellectual property applies and obtains a patent or registers a trade mark or industrial design, the information relating to that intellectual property falls into the public domain and he would be unable to protect it after the period of protection under the relevant law has lapsed. But if he has a secret recipe for example, (such as that for Kentucky Fried Chicken), he can exploit it and protect it indefinitely by keeping it secret. The issue therefore is whether confidential information (or the law of trade secrets as it is known in some jurisdictions) can be used to protect indigenous knowledge.

The three ingredients required to constitute breach of confidence are:
(i)   The information itself must have the quality of confidence about it;
(ii) That information must have been imparted in circumstances importing an obligation of confidence; and
(iii) There must be an authorised use to the detriment of the party communicating it.[9]

A person who has obtained information in confidence is not allowed to use it as a springboard for activities detrimental to the person who made the confidential communication and springboard it remains even when all the features have been published or can be ascertained by actual inspection by any member of the public.[10] The obligation of confidence does not depend on any express or implied contract. It depends on the principle of equity that he who has received information in confidence shall not take unfair advantage of it. He must not make use of it to the prejudice of him who gave it without obtaining his consent.[11]

The obligation of confidence rests not only on the original recipient, but also on any person who received the information with knowledge acquired at the time or subsequently was originally given in confidence.[12] While it is generally an essential ingredient of every copyright action that the plaintiff should start with a work in a permanent form, under the general law of confidence the confidential communication relied on may be either written or oral.[13] This is very important especially in the context of protecting indigenous knowledge. Copyright is good against the world generally, whereas confidence only protects against those who receive information or ideas in confidence. Although copyright has a fixed statutory time limit,[14] and confidence, at all events in theory no time limit, in practice the obligation of confidence ceases the moment information or ideas become public knowledge.[15]

Where there has been a breach of confidence the plaintiff has several remedies. These include: interdict; account of profits; delivery up and destruction; and damages. *Prima facie*, the law of confidential information could effectively protect indigenous knowledge. But a deeper analysis of the three ingredients of the action for breach of confidence reveals that it might not be easy to satisfy the three ingredients for an action for breach of confidence. First, most indigenous knowledge–whether it relates to traditional medicine, music or art–is known not just to one individual but to a group of individuals or even an entire community. In such circumstances, the information is in the public domain and might therefore lack that 'quality of confidence'. Second, when individuals or companies come to developing countries as researchers or in any other guise they collect indigenous knowledge by various methods. Sometimes, they take away plants for further analysis in the developed countries. Most commonly however, they interview members of the community who unwittingly and gratuitously give them all the indigenous knowledge about the particular subject matter. If it is a medicinal plant, the 'researcher' will take it away together with the indigenous knowledge of its medicinal qualities. If a drug is developed from the plant through a combination of further research and the indigenous knowledge, the researcher or the drug company employing him will make millions of dollars but none will be paid to the community and there will not even be an acknowledgment of the contribution of that community in the development of that drug. If the community were to sue the researcher for breach of confidence, it would be very difficult to establish that the information was 'imparted in circumstances importing an obligation of confidence'. Once the second ingredient is not established, it becomes very difficult to establish the third one: once the information is imparted in circumstances which do not import an obligation of confidence, it then becomes difficult to establish 'unauthorised use'. The researcher and the drug company will argue that they did not need the consent of the community or individual who gave them the indigenous knowledge before developing the drug from the plant.

The above analysis shows why it is important to regulate the activities of foreign research - academic or commercial - in any country. This regulatory regime starts with the control of the grant of entry visas, research permits, licensing agreements, and the exportation of indigenous knowledge in any form. As will be shown below, the most important aspect of this regulation is the licensing. The licensing agreement between the community and the researcher (or research team) should expressly impose the obligation of confidence on the researcher; an obligation to acknowledge the contribution of the indigenous community; and an obligation to pay a royalty to the community where the research results in a commercial product such as a drug.

B. Patents

An invention is patentable in Botswana if it is *new, involves an inventive step* and is *industrially applicable*.[16] An application for a patent in respect of an invention may be made by the inventor or by any other person who has acquired from the inventor the right to apply.[17]

It can be seen that although Botswana now has independent patent legislation, indigenous manufacturing processes and methods of treatment would not meet the above criteria if they are to be protected at all.

C. Utility Model Certificates

A utility model is a petty patent or short-term patent. It is a minor technical advance that deserves short-term protection.[18] It can be seen therefore that utility models would be a very good way of protecting of indigenous manufacturing processes and products that do not meet the criteria for a patent. Utility models are protected in Botswana. The law governing patents applies to utility models *mutatis mutandis*.[19]

An invention qualifies for a utility model certificate if it is a new and industrially applicable.[20] The duration of a utility model certificate is seven years. At any time before the grant or refusal of a utility model certificate, an applicant, may, on payment of a prescribed fee, convert his application for a utility model certificate into an application for a patent.[21] It is not entirely clear whether indigenous knowledge in this category would be registerable as utility models.

D. Industrial Designs

What is protected here are the design elements in articles mass produced by an industrial process.[22] An industrial design is capable of registration if it is *new* and *not contrary to public order or morality*.[23] The procedure for application for registration of a design is basically the same as that for the grant of a patent.[24] The duration of the registration of a design is five years, but may on the payment of a renewal fee be renewed for two further consecutive periods of five years.[25]

It would appear that indigenous knowledge in this category would not meet the criteria for registration as industrial designs.

E. Trade Marks

Trade marks are an important aspect of intellectual property. Trade marks and related aspects of trading goodwill are protected as symbols needed by consumers to distinguish between competing products and services in a market economy.[26] An application for the registration of a mark accompanied by the prescribed fee is made to the Registrar of Patents, Marks and Designs in writing with a reproduction of the mark and a list of goods and services for which registration of the mark is requested, listed under the applicable class or classes of the International Classification.[27] Registration gives the owner of a mark exclusive right to the mark in Botswana. No person may use a registered mark unless the owner has authorised him in writing.[28] The rights in a mark may be transferred by cession, assignment, and testamentary disposition or by operation of law.[29] The remedies available for infringement available to the owner of a mark are basically same as those conferred on a patentee.[30] The duration of registration of a mark is ten years but may, on the written request and payment of the prescribed renewal fee by the registered owner, be renewed for consecutive periods of ten years.[31]

It would appear that most indigenous knowledge rights in this category would not qualify for protection as trade marks.

F. Geographical Indications and Appellations of Origin

A geographical indication is a notice stating that a given product originates in a given geographical area. An appellation of origin is a more precise form of geographical indication which specifies that the product has qualities that are derived specifically from the fact that it is made in a particular region.[32] Geographical indications are an important method of indicating the origins of goods and services. One of the aims of their use is to promote commerce by informing the customer of the origin of the product. Often this may imply a certain quality, which the customer may be looking for. They can be used for industrial and agricultural products. The most prominent examples of geographical indications are those used for wines and spirits. For example, the geographical indication 'Champagne' is used to indicate that a special kind of sparkling wine originates in the Champagne region of France. Similarly, 'Cognac' is used for brandy from the French region around the town of Cognac.

The difference between a trade mark and a geographical indication is that a mark is a sign that an individual trader uses to distinguish his own goods or service from the goods or services of his competitors, while a geographical indication is used to show that certain products have a certain origin and can be used by all the producers in that region. For example, 'Stellenbosch' can be used by all wine producers in the Stellenbosch region of South Africa. It can be seen therefore that geographical indications could effectively be used to protect indigenous knowledge products from a particular country or region of a country.

Geographical indications and appellations can be protected nationally as well as internationally. At national level, geographical indications can be protected through legislation or by introducing a register of geographical indications. They can also be protected through the law of unfair competition,[33] or the delict of passing off.[34] Where a trader uses a geographical indication for a product that does not originate in the region named, that amounts to an unfair trade practice.

Geographical indications can also be protected by the registration of collective marks or certification marks. Unlike individual marks, collective marks belong to a group of traders or producers. A certification mark on the other hand does not belong to any particular individual: it is registered on the undertaking that anyone who meets the specified conditions is allowed to use it.

Collective marks and certification marks could be an effective way of protecting indigenous knowledge: producers of artefacts, medicines, drinks, handicrafts, music, food, etc, from a particular community could register a collective mark or certified mark to protect their products from infringement locally and internationally. For example, the weavers from Oodi (Botswana) could register such a mark which would identify and protect their distinctive rugs from infringement anywhere in the world. So too could the potters of Gabane (Botswana) and Thamaga (Botswana).

The Botswana Industrial Property Act 1996 does not specifically refer to geographical indications or to appellations of origin but contains provisions relating to the protection of collective marks. Section 65 provides that the provisions in sections 53-64 relating to marks apply to collective marks. Specific rules relating to collective marks are contained in sections 66 and 67.[35]

At the international level, geographical indications can be protected by bilateral and multilateral arrangements. A country such as South Africa may enter into a bilateral agreement with Botswana for the mutual protection of each country's geographical indications. This would involve the exchange of lists of the geographical indications concerned, and the grant of protection on a reciprocal basis. A multilateral arrangement involves an agreement between several countries. The most prominent one is the Lisbon Agreement for the Protection of Appellations of Origin and their International Registration.

It is submitted that geographical indications and appellations of origins could effectively be used to protect indigenous knowledge within the context of conventional intellectual property law. In the case of Botswana for example, sections 66 and 67 could be amended so as to cater for indigenous knowledge. At the international level, the Lisbon Agreement could also be expanded to accommodate indigenous knowledge.

G. Copyright

This is the most contentious area of intellectual property law in relation to the protection of indigenous knowledge. The object of copyright is to protect creative individuals such as authors and artists from having their work copied or reproduced without their authorisation.[36] Copyright is fundamentally different from a patent, a design or a mark in that legal protection is automatic. This means that a work protected by copyright does not have to be registered with a government agency in order to gain legal protection. Copyright law is concerned with the copying of actual words or other physical material, as opposed to the reproduction of ideas. Copyright is a form of property which may be sold or licensed for use by others, typically by way of contract for the publication of the work.[37]

The British Imperial Copyright Act 1911 was made operable in Botswana by Order in Council.[38] When Britain enacted the Copyright Act, 1956, this too was made operable in Botswana in 1965 by Statutory Instrument.[39] When Botswana became independent in 1966, the British Copyright Act 1956 continued in force.[40] Botswana is a country steeped in oral tradition.[41] The elders have for generations continued the old tradition of relating to their children and grandchildren Tswana folk tales and traditions.[42] Due to the lack of copyright societies, publishing houses and recording studios, most of this folklore has never been recorded.[43] Although the concept of copyright existed in Botswana, the majority of the people never used the term 'copyright' and did not even know what it meant. Most people did not even realise that Botswana had a Copyright Act.[44]

The Botswana Copyright Act 1956 had numerous limitations and shortcomings. It was obscure, bulky, outdated and complicated. It was not suited to Botswana's social and economic conditions and aspirations. Most importantly it did not protect folkloric works, moral rights and neighbouring rights. Botswana required a copyright law which would reflect its social and economic values and aspirations as well as national and international technological developments. By April 1998, Botswana had acceded to the Agreement on the Trade-Related Aspects of Intellectual Property Rights (TRIPS), the

World Intellectual Property Organisation (WIPO) Convention, and the Paris Convention. The ratification of these Conventions and Agreements placed an obligation on Botswana to revise the laws providing for the protection and regulation of copyright so as to bring the levels of protection and type of works protected into line with international standards. These reforms were introduced by the Copyright and Neighbouring Rights Act 2000.

The Copyright and Neighbouring Rights Act 2000

Protected Works

A literary[45] or artistic work[46] is not protected by copyright under the copyright and Neighbouring Rights Act unless it is *an original intellectual creation* in the literary or artistic domain.[47] The types of literary and artistic works protected by the act include:

(a) Books, pamphlets, articles, computer programmes and other writings;

(b) Speeches, lectures, addresses, sermons and other *oral* works;

(c) Dramatic, dramatic-musical works, pantomimes, choreographic works and other works created for stage productions;

(d) Stage productions of works referred to in paragraph (a) and of *expressions of folklore*;

(e) Musical works with or without accompanying words;

(f) Audiovisual works;

(g) Works of *architecture*;

(h) Works of *drawings, painting, sculpture, engraving, lithography, tapestry and other works of fine art*;

(i) Photographic works;

(j) Works of applied art; and

(k) Illustrations, maps, plans, sketches and three-dimensional works relative to geography, typography, architecture or science.[48]

It can be seen that s.3 (2) is very inclusive. Most importantly it protects most of the work that would fall under indigenous knowledge. Expressions of folklore are expressly mentioned. The protection of 'drawings, paintings, sculpture, engraving and tapestry' would cover most of the other indigenous works such as the rock art of the Basarwa; the pottery from different parts of Botswana such as Thamaga and Gabane; the woven mats, carpets, rugs and blankets from Oodi in Botswana and various parts of Lesotho, South Africa and Swaziland. The protection of works of 'architecture' would protect the traditional homes and other architectural works found in many African countries such as Botswana, Egypt, Lesotho, Swaziland and South Africa.

Many musicians and playwrights in Southern Africa have been ripped off for decades due to lack of copyright protection at home and abroad. Artists from abroad have come to Africa, listened to songs of local artists and then returned abroad and recorded modified versions of these songs passing them off as their own. Music producers have done the same. They come to Africa and take away with them recordings of songs by African artists. When they return to the developed countries they reproduce the songs and make millions of dollars without paying royalties to the original composers of these songs in Africa. This is piracy. Such pirated works have raised much concern, particularly in the area of music recordings, as the authors or producers and other owners of the copyright applicable together with their nations have lost considerable amounts of revenue to pirates of copyright. The Copyright and Neighbouring Act 2000 solves this problem by expressly protecting oral works, dramatic, dramatic-musical works with or without accompanying words. Given the fact that Botswana is a party to the international Conventions referred to above, local copyright holders as well as foreign copyright holders from countries that are party to the Conventions are able to enforce their copyright within Botswana, and local copyright holders are able to enforce their copyright in all other countries that are also party to the Conventions.

Rights of the Author

The owner of copyright in a protected work may use the work as he wishes, and may prevent others from using it without his authorisation. The rights given to the author by the Act are exclusive rights. He can authorise others to use the work, subject to the legally recognised rights and interests of others.[49] There are two types of rights under copyright: economic rights,[50] which allow the owner of rights to derive financial gain from the use of his work by others; and moral rights,[51] which allow the author to take certain actions to preserve the personal link between himself and the work.[52]

Neighbouring Rights

Neighbouring rights are the intellectual property rights provided for the protection of the legal interests of certain persons and legal entities who either contribute to making works available to the public or produce subject matter which does not qualify as 'works' under the general understanding of copyright but who nevertheless express creativity or technical and organisational skill sufficient to justify recognition of their contribution as deserving protection.[53] It can therefore be seen that the protection of neighbouring rights is a crucial component in the protection of indigenous knowledge and rights since most of these border on copyright and would not be protected in mainstream copyright law. Neighbouring rights include the rights of performers, producers of sound recordings and broadcasters. The rights of performers[54] are recognised because their creative intervention is necessary to give life, for example, to musical works, dramatic and choreographic works and motion pictures, and because they have a justifiable interest in the legal protection of their individual interpretation.[55] The rights of producers[56] of recordings are recognised because their creative, financial and organisational resources are necessary to make recorded sound available to the public in the form of commercial phonograms such as tapes, cassettes, CDs and Mini Discs. They also have a legitimate interest in having the legal resources necessary to take action against unauthorised uses whether it be through the making and distribution of unauthorised copies (piracy) or in the form of unauthorised broadcasting or communication to the public of their phonograms. The rights of broadcasters[57] are recognised because of their role in making works available to the public, and in the light of their justified interest in controlling the transmission of their broadcasts.[58]

Conclusion

It can be seen that the Botswana Copyright and Neighbouring Act 2000 is a major breakthrough in the protection of copyright in general and indigenous knowledge in particular. Most of the indigenous knowledge rights are protected and the Act contains modern and effective remedies.[59] for the enforcement of rights under the Act. Where it is not possible to provide copyright protection to indigenous knowledge or literary and artistic works due to problems of ownership and originality, the law should then offer protection to the producers and performers of such works under the law of neighbouring rights.

The International Dimension

The World Intellectual Property Organization and the United Nations Educational Scientific Cultural Organisation (UNESCO) are at the forefront of the international protection of indigenous knowledge. At the meeting of WIPO's Governing Bodies in 1978, it was felt that not enough was being done to protect folkloric works.[60] Following that meeting, the International Bureau of WIPO prepared a first draft of *sui generis* model provisions for intellectual property-type protection of folklore against certain unauthorised uses and against distortion.

In 1982, a Committee of Governmental Experts convened by WIPO and UNESCO in Geneva adopted the 'Model Provisions for National Laws on the Protection of Expressions of Folklore against Illicit Exploitation and Other Prejudicial Actions' (hereinafter referred to as 'the Model Provisions').

In 1984 WIPO and UNESCO jointly convened a Group of Experts on the International Protection of Expressions of Folklore by Intellectual Property which met in Paris. The participants had at their disposal a draft treaty based on the Model Provisions and an outline of a similar system of protection at the international level based on the principle of national treatment. However, a number of participants considered it premature to establish an international treaty since there was insufficient experience available as regards the protection of expressions of folklore at the national level, in particular concerning the implementation of the Model Provisions.[61] Two main problems were identified by the Group of Experts: the lack of appropriate sources for identification of expressions of folklore to be protected; and the lack of workable mechanisms for settling of questions of expressions of folklore that are found in more than one country in a given region.[62] Given the lack of agreement at the meeting, the idea of preparing an international treaty was suspended indefinitely.

In 1997, the UNESCO-WIPO World Forum on the Protection of Folklore took place in Phuket, Thailand. At the end of the Forum, an 'Action Plan' was adopted to be submitted to the relevant organs of UNESCO and WIPO. This Action Plan urged both WIPO and UNESCO to pursue efforts to ensure an effective and appropriate international regime for the protection of folklore.

Sub-Programme 11-3 of WIPO's 1998-1999 programme dealt specifically with the protection of folklore. It provided for a number of fact-finding missions and thorough studies, for regional consultations and for active contribution to the establishment of adequate databases and regional co-operative schemes.[63]

In 1999, WIPO, in co-operation with UNESCO, organised four regional consultations: in March in Pretoria for African countries;[64] in April in Hanoi for countries of Asia and the Pacific;[65] in May in Tunisia, for Arab countries;[66] and in June in Quito, for countries of Latin America and the Caribbean.[67] The participants at these meetings supported and urged WIPO in co-operation with UNESCO to continue studies and preparatory work for the establishment and application of appropriate norms for the protection of expressions of folklore at national, sub-regional, regional and international levels. The importance of *collection*, *classification*, *identification* and *documentation* of expressions of folklore was also underlined not only from the viewpoint of their conservation and dissemination but also for the purpose of their intellectual protection.[68]

WIPO's Programme for 2000–2001 expanded on the 1998–1999 Programme. Sub-programme 11.3 was expanded to provide for the convocation of two or three expert meetings to examine alternatives for the development of standards for the protection of folklore at national, regional and international levels. Sub-Programme 11.4 included a pilot project on the possible role of intellectual property in electronic commerce relating to the commercialisation of cultural heritage. This is an issue of great significance for the protection of expressions of folklore given the advent of globalisation and the great strides made in the development of information technology. In 2000, WIPO established the WIPO Intergovernmental Committee on Intellectual Property and Genetic Resources, Traditional Knowledge and Folklore (IGC).

Working in co-operation with other international organisations, WIPO provides a forum for international policy debate concerning the interplay between intellectual property and traditional knowledge and genetic resources. WIPO is also in the process of developing a range of practical tools aimed at enhancing the intellectual property interests of the holders of such knowledge and resources.

Over the last two years, the IGC has laid down a solid basis for WIPO's work in this area, and at its most recent meeting in Geneva in July 2003 explored ideas for future work and considered the prospects for accelerated moves towards concrete outcomes.

The IGC has debated a range of pressing current issues in the field of intellectual property, and has overseen the development of practical tools and mechanisms to support traditional knowledge holders, custodians of traditional culture, and indigenous and local communities in identifying and promoting their interests in relation to the intellectual property system. There has been overall agreement that immediate steps need to be taken to safeguard the interests of those communities which have developed and preserved traditional knowledge and traditional cultures.

The IGC's work has led to a much greater understanding of the issues involved, and the possible approaches to deal with concerns about inadequate recognition and protection of traditional knowledge and cultural expressions. There has been particular acknowledgement of the concerns of communities whose cultural identity and spiritual integrity can depend on how their traditional knowledge and cultural expressions are used and disseminated. The IGC considered steps to enhance the participation of local and indigenous communities in the work of the IGC.[69]

The IGC was mandated by the General Assembly as a forum for discussion of these issues. Since the WIPO General Assembly would need to consider and renew this mandate in September 2003, the IGC's fifth session saw extensive debate about future directions for its work, including moving beyond the initial mandate of serving as a forum for discussion, and a range of proposals on how to build on the substantial foundations it has laid.

There was strong support for the idea that the IGC should move towards concrete outcomes within the next two years, and should focus on the international aspects of protection of traditional knowledge and expressions of folklore or 'traditional cultural expressions' (TCEs). But views differed over the appropriate form and legal status of these outcomes. On the one hand, some delegations felt that the urgent need to respond warranted the conclusion of a legally binding international instrument by 2005; others called for recommendations and principles that would draw together international understanding in the short term and leaving open the possibility of legally binding outcomes in future. A number of NGO participants stressed the need to strengthen and extend international recognition of customary law relating to traditional knowledge (such as the customary laws and protocols that apply within indigenous communities) including a WIPO programme of study on this subject commissioned by the IGC, and to improve the involvement of representatives of indigenous and local communities in any international process.

Improved co-ordination of WIPO's IP-related work in this area with other international processes, including treaty development and implementation on the part of the Convention on Biological Diversity (CBD), the Food and Agriculture Organisation (FAO) and the United Nations Educational, Scientific and Cultural Organisation (UNESCO) was also stressed.

Traditional Knowledge Protection

The IGC continued to foster the exchange of practical understanding of possible approaches for legal protection of traditional knowledge and cultural expressions. A composite study on traditional knowledge protection[70] was prepared for the IGC that covered definitions of traditional knowledge, policy issues in protecting traditional knowledge as intellectual property, and options for specific, or *sui generis*, protection of traditional knowledge. An expert panel at the IGC reviewed a range of *sui generis* mechanisms for traditional knowledge protection, drawing together experts from Costa Rica, Nigeria, Peru, the Philippines, Portugal, the United States and Zambia, which illustrated a range of practical and legal responses that have been developed at national and regional levels. An extensive series of surveys, case studies and analysis of legislation was also prepared for the IGC, to ensure that the IGC's work on traditional knowledge protection is based on a rich understanding of existing approaches and the costs and benefits of different policy options.

Genetic Resources and Traditional Knowledge – Defences Against Ill-founded Patents

The IGC also considered defensive approaches to ensuring that traditional knowledge and genetic resource material are not the subject of illegitimate patent claims (this has led to moves to modify core elements of the patent system, such as the International Patent Classification (IPC) and the basis of international search and examination under the Patent Co-operation Treaty). The International Plant Genetic Resources Institute briefed the IGC on the 'SINGER' database (System-wide Information Network for Genetic Resources) which provides data concerning genetic resources held in trust internationally. This database was recently linked to a WIPO on-line portal that is designed to help patent examiners take greater account of existing traditional knowledge and genetic resources when assessing the validity of patent claims. The IGC also transmitted to the WIPO General Assembly an extensive technical study, requested by the Conference of Parties of the CBD, on the question of disclosure within patent applications of the origin and legal status of genetic resources and traditional knowledge that are used in inventions.[71]

Protection of Expressions of Traditional Culture and Creativity

The IGC considered a composite study on the legal protection of expressions of traditional culture and creativity (or folklore).[72] The ensuing IGC debate highlighted the important policy challenges for new approaches to protection of TCEs - for instance, the contested nature of the notion of the 'public domain', and the concern of many indigenous communities about the way the public domain is conceived in the established IP system, such as when traditional cultural materials are considered under IP law to be in the public domain when in fact customary law or spiritual restrictions on its use may well still apply from the indigenous perspective. Talks have moved to a detailed, practical phase, reflecting the request of the IGC at its last session.

The IGC also considered WIPO's ongoing practical work in this area, including its assistance with the establishment of effective national and regional systems for folklore protection, and development of a 'WIPO Practical Guide on the Legal Protection of Traditional Cultural Expressions'.

Documentation of Traditional Knowledge

Communities in many countries are undertaking a range of programs involving documentation of their traditional knowledge and associated biological resources. These are established for a host of reasons, including preserving traditional knowledge for future generations. But this can fuel concerns that the very process of documentation can undercut the interests of traditional knowledge holders. Unless the right steps are taken in advance, documented traditional knowledge can more readily be accessed, disseminated and used without authorisation, for instance contrary to customary laws and practices. Reflecting these concerns, the IGC noted the further development of a toolkit for managing the IP implications of documentation of traditional knowledge and biological resources.[73] This should heighten awareness of the need to ensure that documentation does not lead to an unintentional loss of rights or of control over traditional knowledge.

The toolkit will clarify practical options for documentation that do not necessarily place the documented material in the public domain when communities wish to retain control over it and limit access, for cultural, spiritual, legal or commercial reasons. Delegates stressed the need to include indigenous and local communities extensively in the development of this toolkit, and underlined that many indigenous communities viewed documentation of traditional knowledge with scepticism. The toolkit will not encourage or promote documentation in itself, but rather ensure that if a community chooses to document their traditional knowledge, for whatever reason, the necessary safeguards are in place to avoid undermining the community's own interests (such as by inadvertently putting traditional knowledge into the public domain).

Latest Developments

The General Assembly of WIPO met in October 2003 in Geneva to consider future directions for the organisation's work in the area of traditional knowledge and genetic resources. The Sixth Session of the IGC is in Geneva in March 2004.[74]

Conclusions

(a) Developing countries must put a higher premium on the protection of indigenous knowledge. Intellectual property law in general and indigenous knowledge in particular, should be put on top of the agenda by such countries in their national laws and in regional and sub-regional arrangements such as the South African Development Community (SADC), the Common Market of Eastern and Southern Africa (COMESA) and the New Economic Partnership for African Development (NEPAD).

(b) While the developed countries saw the value of indigenous knowledge, they were not interested in protecting it. Their only interest was in exploiting it. The dependent intellectual laws they introduced in their colonies were not suited to protecting such knowledge and were never intended to do so. The independent intellectual property laws enacted by developing countries are also in most cases not fully suited to protect indigenous knowledge. There is therefore a need to enact *sui generis* laws that can effectively protect indigenous knowledge. Furthermore there is need for international co-operation to produce an international treaty on indigenous knowledge and to harmonise the law in this area. The final international agreement as well as the national *sui generis* laws must effectively articulate the following:

- *subject matter* to be protected;
- *criteria* for protection;
- *holders* of rights;
- *rights* conferred;
- *procedures* and *formalities* to be followed to obtain protection;
- *responsibilities* of new or existing authorities and institutions;
- *remedies* and *enforcement* procedures;
- *term* of protection;
- interaction of the *sui generis* legislation with existing intellectual property legislation;
- role of customary laws and protocols; and
- Regional and international protection.

(c) WIPO and UNESCO must be commended for their pioneering efforts in the protection of indigenous knowledge. They have worked tirelessly and ceaselessly to produce model laws and agreements on the protection of intellectual property in general and indigenous knowledge in particular. They have assisted various countries financially and otherwise, in the collection, classification, identification and documentation of indigenous knowledge.

(d) Universities in the developing countries such as the University of Botswana must play a major role in protection of indigenous knowledge by educating the relevant communities about indigenous knowledge rights and must be at the forefront in the collection, classification, identification and documentation of indigenous knowledge. It is interesting to note that most Universities in the developed countries have a Department or School of African or Oriental studies while only a few in the developing countries have a Centre or School of African or even European studies.

(e) The best method by which communities can benefit from the legal exploitation of indigenous knowledge is through licensing agreements between the communities that own the indigenous knowledge and companies or organisations that wish to exploit that indigenous knowledge. There is therefore a need to develop Model Licensing Agreements that can be utilised in all developing countries. These agreements should be developed at national and international level. Once again, WIPO, UNESCO, as well as Universities, have a role to play in developing such Model Agreements. The key feature of these licensing Agreements must be adequate and equitable financial compensation to the relevant communities.

(f) Botswana must be commended enacting independent legislation that adequately protects intellectual property rights in general and indigenous knowledge in particular. The Copyright and Neighbouring Rights Act 2000 to a great extent adequately protects indigenous knowledge rights and should serve as a model for those Third World countries that are still striving to enact independent intellectual property legislation. It is hoped that Parliament will soon enact the relevant Rules and Regulations so that the Act might come into force.

Notes

1. A. Briscoe and J. Kiggundu, *A Guide to Intellectual Property Law in Botswana*, (Morula Press, Gaborone, 2001) p.1.
2. Idem.
3. Idem.
4. Laws of Botswana, Chapter 68:01.
5. Ibid, Chapter 68:02.
6. Ibid, Chapter 68:03.
7. Ibid, Chapter 68:04.
8. See further Kiggundu, J., 'The Legal Aspects of Doing Business in Botswana', in *The Legal Aspects of Doing Business in Africa* (Kluwer 2000) p.22.
9. Coco v Clark (A.N.) (Engineers) Ltd [1968] 1 F.S.R. 415; Talbot v General Television [1918] R.P.C.1; Fraser v Evans [1983] 2 All E.R.101.
10. Terrapin Ltd v Builders' Supply Co (Hayes) Ltd & Ors [1967] R.P.C.375; Seager v Copydex (No. 1) [1967] 2 All E.R. 415.
11. Seager v Copydex (No.1) [1967 2 All E.R. 415 (CA). See also Saltman Engineering v Campbell Engineering (1948) 65 R.P.C. 203.
12. Fraser v Thames Television [1982] 2 All E.R. 101.
13. Fraser v Thames Television [1983] 2 All E.R.101.
14. In Botswana the period is the life of the author and fifty years after his death. See further Copyright and Neighbouring Rights Act 2000, s 10.
15. Fraser v Thames Television [1983] 2 All E.R. 101.
16. Industrial Property Act, s.8 (1). See also Kiggundu, op. cit., (note 8) at 23 et seq.
17. Industrial Property Act, s.8 (2).
18. W.R. Cornish, Intellectual Property (3 ed, Sweet & Maxwell, London, 1996) p.9. See also Kiggundu, op cit., (note 16) p.25.
19. Industrial Property Act, s.34.
20. Industrial Property Act, s.35.
21. Industrial Property Act, s.38. See further Kiggundu op cit., (note 18) loc cit.
22. Cornish, W.R. op cit., (note 18) at pp.483 et seq.
23. Industrial Property Act, section 39 (1) and (4).
24. Industrial Property Act, ss.42-49.
25. Ibid, s.49. See further, Kiggundu op cit (note 21) loc cit.
26. Cornish, W.R, op cit., (note 22) p.8. See also Kiggundu op cit., (note 25) loc cit.
27. Industrial Property Act, s.54 (1).
28. Industrial Property Act, s.58 (1).
29. Ibid., s.60.
30. Ibid., s.60.

31. Ibid., s.61.
32. See Briscoe and Kiggundu op. cit. (note 1) pp.8-9. On geographical indications generally, see M.A. Nicholas, 'Geographical indications for Foods, Trips and the Doha Development Agenda', 2003, 47, J.A.L., 199.
33. On which see Briscoe and Kiggundu, op cit., (note 32) pp.10-12.
34. Passing off is a delict which occurs where a person suggests or creates the impression that his business undertaking is that of another. In order to succeed in a passing off action, a plaintiff has to establish three elements: reputation; a misrepresentation; and a likelihood of damage. See Reckitt & Coleman v Borden [1990] R.P.C. 341 at 406 (per Lord Oliver). Lord Oliver's trinity of elements in the Reckitt case is to be preferred to the House of Lords' five in Warnink v Townend [1979] A.C. 731 (per Lord Diplock and Lord Fraser of Tullybelton). See further Briscoe and Kiggundu op cit (note 33) at 11-12.
35. Under section 66, the Registrar of Marks, Patents and Designs may invalidate the registration of a collective mark if (inter alia) the person requesting such invalidation proves that only the registered owner uses the mark, or that he uses or permits its use in a manner which is liable to deceive trade circles, or the public as to the origin or any other common characteristics of the goods or services concerned. Under section 67 (3), the registration of a collective mark, or an application therefore, may not be the subject of a license contract.
36. See Briscoe and Kiggundu op cit., (note 33) p.16.
37. Briscoe and Kiggundu op cit., (note 36) loc cit.
38. No. 35 of 1912.
39. The Copyright (Bechuanaland) Order 1965 (S.I 1965/2009).
40. See the Botswana Independence Act 1966 (Cap 23) and the Botswana Independence Order (S.I 1966/117). This is an example of dependent legislation continuing in force after independence.
41. Segopolo, S.M.A., 'Development and Current Status of Copyright Protection in Botswana', (WIPO/CNR/GBE/97/2) p. 3.
42. Idem.
43. Idem.
44. Idem.
45. 'Literary work' means any work, other than a dramatic or musical work, which is written, spoken or sung, and accordingly includes a table of compilation and a computer programme. See Copyright and Neighbouring Rights Act 200, s.2.
46. 'Artistic work' means: (a) a graphic work, photograph, sculpture or collage, irrespective of its artistic quality; (b) a work of architecture being a building or a model of a building irrespective of its artistic quality; and (c) a work of artistic craftsmanship not falling within paragraph (a) or (b) irrespective of its artistic quality: see Copyright and Neighbouring Rights Act 2000, s.2.
47. Copyright and Neighbouring Rights Act 2000, s.3 (1).
48. Copyright and Neighbouring Rights Act, s.3 (2). The Minister of Trade and Industry may by Orders add to or otherwise vary this list of works, s.3 (3). Moreover, under s.4 of the same Act derivative works are also given copyright protection. These

are: translations, adaptations, arrangements and other transformations or modifications of works; and collections of works, collections of mere data (databases) whether in machine readable or other form, and collections of expression of folklore, provided that such collections are original by reason of the selection, co-ordination or arrangement of their contents.

49. Briscoe and Kiggundu, op cit., (note 37) p.17.

50. See Copyright and Neighbouring Rights Act 2000, s.7. The author or other owner of copyright has the exclusive right to carry out or authorise any of the following acts in relation to the work:

- Reproduction of the work;
- Translation of the work;
- Adaptation, arrangement or other transformation of the work;
- The first public distribution of the original and each copy of an audiovisual work, a work embodied in sound recording, a computer programme, a database or a musical work in the form of notation, irrespective of the ownership of the original or copy concerned;
- Importation of copies of the work, even where the imported copies were made with the authorisation of the author or other owner of copyright;
- Public display of the original or a copy of the work;
- Public performance of the work;
- Broadcasting of the work;
- Other communication to the public of work (this covers cable and internet distribution). See further Briscoe and Kiggundu op cit., (note 49) pp.18-19.

51. Ibid., s.8.

52. Briscoe and Kiggundu, op cit., (note 39) p.17.

53. Briscoe and Kiggundu, op cit., (note 52) p.20.

54. See Copyright and Neighbouring Rights Act 2000, s.24.

55. Briscoe and Kiggundu, op cit., (note 53) loc cit.

56. See Copyright and Neighbouring Rights Act 2000, s.25.

57. See Copyright and Neighbouring Rights Act 2000, s.27.

58. Briscoe and Kiggundu, op cit., (note 55) loc cit.

59. The remedies in the Copyright and Neighbouring Rights Act 2000 can be divided into the following categories: conservatory or provisional measures; civil remedies; criminal sanctions; measures to be taken at the border; and measures, remedies and sanctions against abuses in respect of technical devices. Conservatory or provisional measures (s.29) have two purposes: first, to prevent infringements from occurring, particularly to prevent the entry of infringing goods into the channels of commerce, including entry of imported goods after clearance by customs; and second, to preserve relevant evidence in regard to an alleged infringement. Thus, judicial authorities may have the authority to order that provisional measures be carried out without advance notice to the alleged infringer. In this way, the alleged infringer is prevented from relocating the suspected infringing materials to avoid detection. The most common provisional measure is a search of the premises of the alleged infringer and seizure of suspected infringing

goods, the equipment used to manufacture them, and all relevant documents and other records of the alleged infringing business activities.

Civil remedies (s.30) compensate the owner of rights for economic injury suffered because of the infringement, usually in the form of monetary damages, and create an effective deterrent to further infringement, often in the form of judicial order to destroy the infringing goods and the materials and implements which have been predominantly used for producing them; where there is a danger that infringing acts may be continued, the court may also issue injunctions against such acts, failure to comply with which would subject the infringer to payment of a fine.

Criminal sanctions (s.31) are intended to punish those who wilfully commit acts of piracy of copyright and neighbouring rights on a commercial scale, and, as in the case of civil remedies, to deter further infringement. The purpose of punishment is served by the imposition of substantial fines, and by sentences of imprisonment consistent with the level of penalties applied for crimes of corresponding seriousness, particularly in cases of repeat offences. The purpose of deterrence is served by orders for the seizure, forfeiture and destruction of infringing goods, as well as the materials and implements the predominant use of which has been to commit the offence.

Measures to be taken at the border (s.32) are different from the enforcement measures described so far, in that they involve action by the customs authorities rather than by the judicial authorities. Border measures allow the owner of rights to apply to customs authorities to suspend the release into circulation of goods which are suspected of infringing copyright. The purpose of the suspension into circulation is to provide the owner of rights a reasonable time to commence judicial proceedings against the suspected infringer, without the risk that the alleged infringing goods will disappear into circulation following customs clearance. The owner of rights must generally satisfy the customs authorities that there is prima facie evidence of infringement, must provide detailed description of the goods so that they may be recognised, and must provide a security to indemnify the importer, the owner of the goods, and the customs authorities in case the goods turn out to be non-infringing.

The final category of enforcement provisions, which has achieved greater important in the advent of digital technology, includes measures, remedies and sanctions against abuses in respect of technical means (s.33). In certain cases, the only practical means of preventing copying is through so-called 'copy-protection' or 'copy-management' systems, which contain technical devices that either prevent entirely the making of copies or make the quality of the copies so poor that they are unusable. Technical devices are also used to prevent the reception of encrypted commercial television programmes except with the use of decoders. However, it is technically possible to manufacture devices by means of which copy-protection and copy-management systems, as well as encryption systems, may be circumvented. The theory behind provisions against abuse of such devices is that their manufacture, importation and distribution should be considered infringements of copyright to be sanctioned in ways similar to other violations.

60. See M. Ficsor, 'Indigenous Peoples and Local Communities: Exploitation of Issues Related to Intellectual Property Protection of Expressions of Traditional Culture', in ATRIP, Collection of Papers Presented at the ATRIP Annual Meeting (Geneva 7-9, 1991) p.35 and p.40.

61. See Ficsor, op cit., (note 60) p.46.

62. Ficsor, op cit., (note 61) p.47.

63. Ficsor, op cit., (note 62) p.48. Sub-programme 11.1 set out as its objective 'to identify and explore the intellectual property needs and expectations of... holders of indigenous knowledge and innovations, in order to promote the contribution of intellectual property to the social, cultural and economic development'. Sub-Programme 11.2 addressed the issues of biological diversity and biotechnology. See further Ficsor, idem.

64. See document WIPO-UNESCO/FOLK/AFR/199/1.

65. See document WIPO-UNESCO/FOLK/ASIA/99/1.

66. See document WIPO-UNESCO/FOLK/ARAB/99/1.

67. See document WIPO-UNESCO/FOLK/LAC/99/1.

68. Fiscor, op cit., (note 52) at 51.

69. See document WIPO/GRTKF/IC/5/11.

70. See document WIPO/GRTKF/IC/5/8.

71. See document WIPO/GRTKF/IC/5/10.

72. See document WIPO/GRTKF/IC/5/3.

73. See document WIPO/GRTKF/IC/5/8.

74. For a further review of the IGC's work to date, see documents IPO/GRTKF/IC/5/INF/3;WIPO/GRTKF/IC/5/INF/4;and WIPO/GRTKF/IC/5/8.

4

Protecting Folklore under Modern Intellectual Property Regimes: Limitations and Alternative Regimes for Protection

Siamisang Morolong

Introduction

Over the last quarter of a century there has been unprecedented activity in the area of the legal protection of folklore, with developing countries, indigenous communities and custodians of folklore calling for its legal protection by intellectual property laws (Kutty Valsala 2002: iii)). Developing countries and indigenous communities consider folklore as an important component of their cultural heritage and perceive the threats posed by its improper exploitation a matter of grave concern (Kutty Valsala 2002: iii)). They have lamented the fact that their folklore is not adequately protected under the existing system of intellectual property rights (Daes 1998; Thebe 1999).

This paper examines the efficacy of conventional intellectual property regimes in the protection of folklore and explores the possibility of using alternative regimes to complement the intellectual property regime or to supplement it where it is lacking.

What is Folklore?

Folklore is recognised as an important element of the cultural heritage of every nation (WIPO 1998a). Folklore has been defined as 'the sum total of human creativity' (Kutty Valsala 2002:7). It is said to encompass 'the customs, games, beliefs, festivals, and practices which human societies have owned through tradition from generation to generation' (Kutty Valsala 2002: 7). It includes folk literature such as myths, legends, fairytales, anecdotes, short stories, proverbs, riddles, rhymes etc. It also includes folk practices including folk beliefs, customs, superstitions, rites and rituals folk games and folk sports (Kutty Valsala 2002: iii). Folklore further encompasses folk arts or artistic folklore which includes folk dance, folk gestures, embroidery, weaving, and carpet making costume designing (Kutty Valsala 2002: iii). Lastly it encompasses what has been broadly termed folk science and technology which includes folk medicines, preparation of dairy products, fertilizers, methods of agriculture, folk architecture, tool making and ornament making and pottery (Kutty Valsala 2002: iii). Folklore tends to be passed on from generation to generation within a community, from memory, by word of mouth or visually (Kutty Valsala 2002: iii). In many countries folklore is a living and still developing tradition, and is not confined to the past (Ficsor 1999; Kutty Valsala 2002; WIPO 1998a).

Reasons Advanced for Intellectual Property Protection of Folklore

Calls for the protection of expressions of folklore have been made on numerous grounds. It has been contended that as intellectual property seeks to reward and protect creativity, expressions of folklore as a manifestation of intellectual creativity deserve to be accorded the same legal protection and status that is accorded to other forms of intellectual property. Communities who are bearers and custodians of cultural heritage argue that while they are unable to acquire intellectual property protection over their cultural heritage, others from outside the community are able to acquire protection for creations derived from this cultural heritage (WIPO 2003:51). They argue that recognising folkloric creations as intellectual property would give them greater control over their use.

The complaint is that folkloric creations, belonging to developing countries and indigenous communities, are often distorted or mutilated in order to adapt them to the needs of western markets (Ficsor 1999; Valsala 2002). For instance the folklore of many communities has been appropriated and wrongly used by outsiders. Performances of songs and dances by traditional and indigenous communities have been recorded and subsequently reproduced on electronic media such as the Internet (Janke 2002). It is common today to find art and other objects imported from traditional communities being sold in shops and other areas. Record companies and performing groups are sampling indigenous music and dance, and these works are presented to the public as original copyright works of those record companies or their associates (Janke 2002). Some individuals and companies have registered 'folkloric themes and words such as 'Pontiac', 'Cherokee', 'Rooibos' and others a (WIPO 2003:33). Traditional instruments have been transformed into modern instruments, renamed and commercialised, or used by non-traditional persons in the world music community or for purposes of tourism (Sandler 2001).

This improper use of folklore is said to have been augmented by the development of new technology and electronic media such as television, the Internet, CD-ROMS etc. These new technologies have generated newer ways for cultural products to be created, replicated and exchanged (Kutty Valsala 2002). For instance it is now possible to download traditional music from free music archives onto ones' home computer and have it stored as digital information that can be transferred into other sound files (that is new compositions) where it can be manipulated in whatever manner one sees fit (Sandler 2001: 58-59). Thus, it has been argued that these new technologies have made the need for the protection of expressions of folklore all the more imperative (WIPO 1998b; Oman 1997).

Others advocate for the intellectual property protection of folklore simply on the basis of reciprocity. They contend that developing countries are pressured to grant intellectual property protection to rights that are important to the developed nations such as patents, trademarks and copyrights, and yet developed countries fail to reciprocate by protecting what is important to developing countries and indigenous communities. The argument therefore is that folklore should be placed on an equal footing as other intellectual property rights, which are imposed on the global community in terms of the Agreement of Trade-Related Aspects of Intellectual Property Rights (TRIPS) which requires members of the World Trade Organisation to comply with the standards that are stipulated in TRIPS on patents, trademarks, copyright, industrial designs and unfair competition.

Problems with Protecting Folklore under General (Conventional) Intellectual Property Laws

As previously indicated, intellectual property law seeks to protect the creations of the human mind and intellect. The Convention Establishing the World Intellectual Property Organisation (WIPO) concluded at Stockholm on 14 July, 1967 states in Article 2 that:

[I]ntellectual Property includes rights relating to:

- Literary/artistic and scientific works;

- Performances of performing artists, phonograms and broadcasts;

- Inventions in all fields of human endeavour;

- Scientific discoveries;

- Industrial designs;

- Trademarks, service marks, and commercial names and designations;

- Protection against unfair competition.

No mention is made of folklore, or expressions of folklore or traditional cultural expressions in this definition. What has become apparent over the years is that there are inherent difficulties in fitting some aspects of folklore into the above categories because of certain accepted notions of intellectual property. As has been observed:

> it is difficult to classify indigenous knowledge innovations and practices into categories of intellectual property developed for use by commercial firms in an industrial and secular context because the lines between indigenous, religious, cultural, business, intellectual and physical property are not as distinct or mutually exclusive. For instance indigenous sacred sites are frequently both ecological reserves developed through human knowledge of management and conservation and cultural centres that have both physical as well as spiritual significance (Posey et al., 1993: 2).

The difficulty of protecting folklore by intellectual property rights arises firstly from the fact that intellectual property laws reflect a bias in favour of individuals who are said to own rights in the protected works. The essence of intellectual property rights is to establish private property rights in creations and innovations in order to grant control over their exploitation and to produce incentives for further creativity and dissemination of the products of human creativity. On the other hand:

> [i]ndigenous people do not view their heritage in terms of property at all but in terms of community and individual responsibility. Possessing a song, story or medical knowledge carries with it certain responsibilities to show respect to, and maintain a reciprocal relationship with, the human beings, animals, plants and places with which the song, story, or medicine is connected (Daes 1998:308).

An aboriginal indigenous artist has captured this sense of communal ownership where he stated as follows:

> As an artist, while I may own the copyright in a particular art work under western law, under aboriginal law I must not use an image or a story in such a way as to undermine the rights of all the other [members of my clan] who have an interest whether direct or indirect in it. In this way I hold the image in trust for all other [clan members] (WIPO 2003:36).

The legislation of many African countries underscores this thinking that folklore is communally owned. For example the Copyright and Neighbouring Rights Act, 2000 of Botswana in section 2 defines expressions of folklore as: 'a group oriented and tradition based creation of groups or persons reflecting the expectation of the community as an adequate expression of its cultural and social identity, its standards and values, as transmitted orally, by imitation or by other means...' The Copyright Act of Nigeria has an identical definition (Asein 1998).

Attempts to determine ownership of folklore in the intellectual property sense may further be complicated by the fact that some creations are common to ethnic groups spanning several countries. Further the creation of intellectual property-type rights over folklore may actually stifle the ability of indigenous and traditional persons in creating and innovating based upon tradition as intellectual property creates exclusivity and monopoly rights. Members of the cultural communities would not be able to create new works based on cultural heritage if private property rights are established over it.

Secondly, it is difficult to protect folklore under intellectual property rights because of certain requirements for protection such as novelty, inventiveness, originality and duration of protection. These limitations are discussed in more detail below under the various categories of intellectual property.

Limitations of Protecting Folklore under the Copyright System

Copyright relates to artistic creations such as poems, novels, music and paintings. The goal of copyright protection is to protect the works of creators from copying and other activities such as communication to the public. What is protected however is the expression and not the ideas underlying the expression.

Copyright protects literary and artistic works in terms of article 2(1) of the Berne Convention on the protection of Literary and Artistic Works (the Berne Convention). In terms of the Berne Convention all productions in the literary, scientific and artistic domain are covered by copyright, irrespective of the manner of expression. Proponents of intellectual property protection of folklore have indicated that many aspects of folklore such as traditional paintings, sculptures, drawings, dramas and dances, and folk song and folktales would fit in this definition of copyright.

The first attempts to regulate the use of creations of folklore were made within the framework of copyright laws with many African countries enacting provisions within their copyright laws to protect folklore. In 1976, the United Nations Educational Scientific and Cultural Organisation (UNESCO) and WIPO came up with the Tunis Model Copyright Law (Tunis Model Law). The Tunis Model Law was to be used as a guideline in drafting national copyright legislation. The Tunis Model law sought to protect folklore to ensure the prevention of 'any improper exploitation and to permit adequate protection of the cultural heritage known as folklore which constitutes not only a potential for economic expansion, but also a cultural legacy intimately bound up with the individual character of the community'.

The Tunis Model Provisions define folklore in section 18 as 'all literary, artistic and scientific works created on national territory by authors presumed to be nationals of such countries or by ethnic communities, passed from generation to generation and constituting one of the basic elements of the traditional cultural heritage'. The Tunis Model Laws provide for protection of works of national folklore, for an indefinite period, whether or not the expression of folklore is fixed in a material form.

The Model law also creates moral and economic rights to be administered by a competent authority established by the state. Fees collected by this authority in exchange for the use of folklore are to benefit the community,

The Tunis Model Laws influenced significantly the copyright laws of number of African countries with many countries referring to folklore in their national copyright legislation.

At the international level an attempt was made to protect folklore by means of copyright by the Diplomatic Conference of Stockholm in 1967. This was done by inserting Article 15(4) in the Berne Convention which provides that:

(a) In the case of unpublished works where the identity of the author is unknown and there is every ground to presume that he is a national of a country of the union, it shall be matter for the legislation in that country to designate the competent authority which shall represent the author and shall be entitled to protect and enforce his rights in the countries of the Union.

(b) Countries of the Union which make such designations under the terms of this provision shall notify the Director General of WIPO by means of a written declaration giving full information concerning the authority thus designated. The Director General shall at once communicate this declaration to all countries of the union.

This Article is interpreted as providing for the possibility of protecting expressions of folklore. It must be noted, however, that nothing in the Article indicates that the provision has anything to do with folklore but it has been said that even though there is no mention '[of] the word folklore which was considered to be extremely difficult to define, the provisions apply to all works fulfilling the conditions It is clear, however, that the main field of application of this regulation will coincide with those productions which are generally described as folklore' (Ficsor 1999: 4).

Ficsor (1999) notes that the Berne provisions have never been invoked by any member and he says that this points to their inadequacy. They have been criticised as they are said to assimilate folklore with ordinary literary and artistic works protected under copyright (Ficsor 1999: 6-7). The view is that 'protection under copyright law is not the answer to the question of how to preserve community owned cultural heritage expressed as folklore' (Ficsor1999: 6). This is due to the fact that requirements for protection of copyright are at variance with rules governing the creation and utilisation of folklore in many communities.

The difficulty in protecting expressions of folklore arises from the fact that copyright law requires that the work be original. Originality requires that the work originate from the author in the sense that he has expended sufficient labour judgement or skill in the creation of the work and has not slavishly copied it from elsewhere. Generally folklore creations tend to be inspired by pre-existing traditions and successive patterns of imitation over time, and this means that the copyright requirement of originality would not be satisfied. Thus expressions of folklore are often excluded from copyright protection since their originality is difficult to establish.

The second difficulty is that copyright systems vest copyright in the owner or author of the work. Most expressions of folklore are linked with the identity of indigenous communities, are handed down from generation to generation, and are said to be collectively owned by the community. Folklore works tend to be the result of collective efforts, and often no one individual can solely be identified as the author of a design, song, dance or other manifestation of folklore. Given the passage of folklore through generations of people in the community, it is difficult to identify any particular individual as the author. Whilst an individual may have created the work, it would eventually have been acquired and used by the society at large and gradually with the passage of time, it loses its individualistic traits as often the original creator of the work cannot be identified.

The third limitation is that copyright protection is for a limited duration. Protection is linked to the lifetime of the author, or to date of fixation, performance or publication. The concern for developing countries, indigenous communities, and custodians of folklore is that folkloric works protected for the duration specified in copyright systems could end up in the wrong hands once the copyright expires and the resultant effect of this would be to rob the rightful owners of the cultural heritage.

Another requirement that has been introduced by legislation of various countries is that for copyright to accrue to a work, the work must have been written down, recorded or otherwise reduced to a material form—the requirement of fixation. Some folkloric works such as songs and dances would not satisfy this requirement.

Limitations of Protecting Folklore under the Patent System

Advocates for the expansion of intellectual property to folklore contend that some aspects of folklore such as technological processes involved in cloth weaving, metal working or constructing musical instruments and the practice of herbal medicines can be patented. To obtain a patent three requirements must be met. The invention must be new, must involve an inventive step, and must be industrially applicable. Many traditional methods are capable of a technological use but they are unlikely to meet statutory criteria pertaining to novelty, as they are already available to the public. The patent system requires refinement of the product and process in order to indicate novelty and to indicate what is claimed in the patent specification. The patent system requires disclosure of the information. Some of the processes involved in traditional use of folklore require secrecy and would therefore not satisfy this requirement. Patents give protection for a limited term of years. Thus the term of protection in here is plagued by the same limitation stated under copyright.

Limitations of Protecting Folklore as Industrial Designs

An industrial design is the ornamental or aesthetic aspect of a functional or useful article. The design must appeal to the sense of sight, i.e., be visually significant, it must be reproducible by industrial means, and the design must not be dictated by function. Industrial design law protects the external appearance of independently created functional items. The duration of protection for industrial designs is ten years, which may be renewed. The design right holder has a right to prevent others from reproducing, selling, importing articles, which embody the same, or similar, design. For protection to arise the design must be shown to be new or novel.

Some traditional designs would not satisfy this novelty requirement because they have been in the public domain since time immemorial. The requirement of novelty therefore can present difficulties for those traditional designs that are already in the public domain. Indigenous peoples and traditional communities desire to protect their traditional designs against exploitation by non-indigenous persons indefinitely, and the limited term of protection offered by industrial design rights is deemed to be unsatisfactory.

Limitations of Protecting Folklore under Trademark Law

It has been contended that aspects of folklore such as clothing designs, sophisticated marks on agricultural implements and carvings could be protected as trademarks. A trademark is any visible sign capable of distinguishing the goods and services of one enterprise from another. It is a sign used on or in connection with the marketing of goods. A trademark performs four main functions: firstly, it serves to distinguish the products or services of one enterprise from products or services of other enterprises; secondly, trademarks give indications as to the origin of the goods or services; thirdly, trademarks refer to particular quality of goods; and fourthly, they promote the marketing of the goods and services.

Janke (2002) has observed that in Australia a number of aboriginals have registered various words and marks as trademarks (pp.14-15). Developing countries, indigenous and traditional peoples have, however, raised concerns that the trademark system does not meet their needs because of the requirement that trademarks be used in the course of trade (Janke 2002). This requirement entails that the folkloric work to be protected by trademarks must be used in the course of trade. This does not assist traditional cultural communities who only wish to protect their words and other marks against exploitation and do not desire to use them in trade.

Unfair Competition and Folklore

Article 10 *bis* of the Paris Convention proscribes acts of unfair competition. These are said to include:

- Acts which may cause confusion with the products or services, or the industrial or commercial activities of a competitor;

- False allegations which may discredit the products or services, or the industrial or commercial activities of a competitor,

- Indications or allegations which may mislead the public, in particular as to the manufacturing process of a product or as to the quality, quantity or other characteristics of products or services.

Unfair competition laws challenge the sale of fake copies of works. They prohibit deceptive practices in marketing and sales and may be relevant for the protection of expressions of folklore by preventing the sale of fake copies of folklore. However it has been argued that it is not feasible to protect folklore under unfair competition laws because of the narrow scope of prohibited acts. Unfair competition laws are concerned with misrepresentations relating to commercial goods or services and they may not be useful in the protection of some types of folklore not meeting this criterion, such as rituals and dance.

Limitations of Protecting Folklore under Trade secrets Law/Breach of Confidence

Article 39 of the TRIPS agreement requires the protection of undisclosed information/trade secrets from unlawful acquisition, disclosure or use in a manner contrary to honest commercial practices. To sustain an action for breach of confidence three main elements must be shown to exist. Firstly the information must be confidential, secondly there must be an obligation to keep the information confidential, and thirdly there must be unauthorised use of the information.

It has been suggested that trade secrets law should be used for protecting folklore that has a spiritual significance and that has been revealed only to properly initiated clan members, as well as to protecting sacred designs. In the Australian case of *Foster v Mountford* (1976) 29 FLR, sacred information was protected as confidential information. The case involved the sale of a book written by Dr Mountford containing sacred knowledge divulged to him by tribal leaders. The book included photographs and descriptions of secret ceremonies. The court held that the information was of deep religious and cultural significance to the tribe. The court then decided that the information had been communicated to Dr Mountford under circumstances importing a duty of confidentiality and therefore that the publication of the book amounted to breach of confidence.

Neighbouring Rights Law

Neighbouring Rights are rights which are related to and are said to be neighbouring on copyright. Neighbouring rights give protection to those who assist copyright owners or authors to communicate their message and disseminate their works to the public. There are three kinds of neighbouring rights: (i) the rights of performing artists in their performances, (ii) the rights of producers of phonograms (sound recordings) in their phonograms; and (iii) the rights of broadcasting organisations in their radio and television programmes.

It has been suggested that many categories of folklore can be protected indirectly by neighbouring rights law. These would include folk tales, folk poetry, folk songs instrumental folk music, folk dances, folk plays and similar expressions. Protection here would arise by affording protection to the performers of such folklore and by so doing the performances of such expressions of folklore also enjoy protection. Such a protection is indirect because what is protected is not the folklore proper but the performers, producers, or broadcasting organisations over their performances or sound recordings.

Neighbouring rights, however, cannot fully satisfy the need for protection against improper use of folklore since they cannot prevent the copying of expressions of folklore, which are not performed, broadcast or contained in a phonogram. Furthermore the limited duration of protection of neighbouring rights does not fit folklore for the same reason as stated for all other intellectual property rights discussed above.

Conclusion

As can be seen from the foregoing, conventional intellectual property regimes do not adequately protect expressions of folklore. Conventional intellectual property rights are based on concepts of individual ownership. Furthermore other aspects of conventional intellectual property systems make it difficult to protect folklore. These are the notions of novelty and other requirements for protection. The inadequacies in the conventional have led to the condemnation of the prevailing system of intellectual property by developing countries and many indigenous groups who see the system as colonialist, racist and as a form of usurpation. Developing countries and indigenous communities have now begun a political struggle to change the existing intellectual property regime (Drahos 1998).

Alternative Regimes for the Protection of Expressions of Folklore

Given the inadequacies of the intellectual property regimes highlighted above, a number of alternatives to the intellectual property regime have been suggested for the protection of intellectual property rights. This section discusses some of those suggestions.

Moral Rights

The moral rights concept of copyright is regarded as being potentially useful for the protection of folklore and traditional knowledge (WIPO 2001). Moral rights are rights given to owners/authors of works to object to derogatory treatment of their work as well as to any false attribution. They are aimed at maintaining the integrity of the author's work. The use of moral rights in folklore would be useful in protecting the work from debasement, mutilation and destruction.

However, moral rights would be difficult to enforce in the case of folklore because they are plagued by the same limitations as other concepts of intellectual property law. Moral rights, like intellectual property laws, are concerned with protecting the reputation or interests of an individual rather than the community.

Customary Laws

It has been suggested that customary laws and practices should be taken into account to ensure the proper protection and preservation of folklore. During WIPO's fact-finding missions on the protection of traditional knowledge, persons consulted alluded to customary regimes or protocols to protect and regulate traditional knowledge and folklore. An example was given of customary norms in Uganda, where according to custom, folk songs are classified according to their nature and uses, and are restricted to those uses; musical instruments are said to be divided into those that can be played by the monarchy and those that can be played by commoners; traditional dances are divided into various categories such as wedding dances, funeral dances etc., and can only be performed within their customary context (WIPO 2001: 92).

During this fact-finding mission, one commentator stated that: 'we have had songs, traditional knowledge and so on for hundreds of years. There was no doubt as to who originally owned them... There were clear customary laws regarding the rights to use songs and the knowledge. There was no problem in the past. Why are there problems now? We should begin with communities and see how communities protected their cultural expressions and knowledge. Then we should use the same customary tools or tools adapted from them' (WIPO, 2001: 76).

Customary norms are often not effective because they lack proper enforcement mechanisms. Another problem is that foreigners are the ones who engage in the appropriation of IKS, and customary norms often do not apply to them as they are not members of the community. For example, in Botswana customary law can only be applied to tribesmen and not to foreigners.

Domain Public Payant

It has been suggested that the doctrine of domain public payant be utilised to ensure the protection of folklore (WIPO 2001). The doctrine of domain public payant allows the use of works that have entered the public domain in return for the payment of royalties. The doctrine refers to a system where the works of unidentified authors can be exploited subject to the payment of fees to the state. Under this system, indigenous folklore works in the public domain would generate revenue for the communities who own them. This system however does not protect against the debasing of culturally sensitive information. It is said to also create the impression that such folklore is available for general use, albeit for a fee.

Droit de Suite

The *droit de suite* is a kind of resale royalty giving the creator of a work the right to share in the increased value of the work if it is later resold or gives rise to a windfall gain. Indigenous folk art has generated great interest and attracts high prices; this system would allow the collection of any windfall gain derived from the sale or resale of folklore to be used for the benefit of the community (WIPO 2001).

Contract Laws
It has been suggested that folklore should be protected through contractual arrangements. Contract law is seen as providing some advantages over intellectual property. Contractual rights can vest in a group and can be of extended duration. The contract would clearly stipulate the conditions relating to the use of the folklore material as well as other issues such as commercial return to the communities and licensing. The limitation of using contractual arrangements is that the benefits flow to the custodians of culture or to the indigenous communities only if the government or non-governmental organisations so desire. The potential for abuse of folklore by foreigners still remains, even under contractual arrangements.

Human Rights Laws
It has been suggested that human rights instruments be invoked to ensure protection of expressions of folklore. The existing human rights instruments do not explicitly provide for the protection of folklore and traditional knowledge, but it has been said that some of the provisions can be utilised to ensure their protection. The 1948 Universal Declaration of Human Rights (UDHR) contains such provisions. Article 27 of the UDHR provides that: 'Everyone has a right to freely participate in the cultural life of the community, to enjoy the arts and to share in scientific advancement and its benefits'. This provision has been said to provide a basis for 'indigenous and local peoples to be entitled to benefits arising from the use of their knowledge and resources' (Mugabe 1998). Article 27(2) of the UDHR provides that: '[e]veryone has the right to protection of the moral and material interests resulting from any scientific, literary or artistic production of which he is the author'. It has been contended that this provision can be implicitly used to grant indigenous and local communities and developing countries protection in respect of the moral, cultural, and material interests in their traditional knowledge and folklore (Mugabe 1998). However, there are limitations in using the UDHR to protect folklore and traditional knowledge. Whilst folklore and 'traditional knowledge is collective property and generates collective rights, the UDHR largely provides for individual rights' (Mugabe 1998: 112). The assertion is that collective rights are not human rights and cannot therefore be protected by human rights instruments.

The International Covenant on Economic, Social and Cultural Rights also provides provisions that can be interpreted to protect the interests over folklore and traditional knowledge. Article 1 thereof 'establishes the right of self determination, including the right to dispose of natural wealth and resources. This implies the right to protect and conserve resources including intellectual property' (Posey1994:125). The Convention on Biological Diversity and the

ILO Convention Concerning Indigenous Peoples in Independent Countries are other examples of international conventions that contain provisions that can be invoked to protect folklore and traditional knowledge. Human rights however remain of limited utility in the protection of expressions of folklore because they are directed mainly at state governments and establish no clear basis for application to corporations or persons involved in the unauthorised utilisation of folklore.

Documentation of Expressions of Folklore
Another method suggested is the documentation and recording of traditional expressions and indigenous peoples' cultures. The suggestion is that communities undertake to keep records and documentation of their expressions of folklore and culture. An example of documentation efforts is the Oman Centre of Traditional Music in Muscat, Oman, which has documented Oman's musical traditions, audiovisual recordings and sound recordings (WIPO 2001:102). In India, the Society for Research Initiatives for Sustainable Technologies has developed databases of traditional knowledge and innovations in close collaboration with members of the local community (Thebe 1999).

Documentation, however, has been opposed by others on the grounds that it makes the folklore more accessible and available and could undermine the efforts of communities to protect it. Delegates at the ARIPO-EPO-UK Patent Office Conference held in Botswana from 16 to 18 October 2001 were averse to the creation of databases to document folklore and traditional knowledge on the grounds that it would create a springboard for western countries to use the documents to advance their own interests. Communities have also raised the concern of the possibility of breaches of confidentiality between ethnographers and informants and the possibility of misrepresentation of indigenous and traditional cultures as well as lack of access to documentary materials by the people about whom the documentation was conducted.

Sui Generis Regimes
It has been suggested that a *sui generis* system of intellectual property should be developed which is specifically adapted to the nature and characteristics of expressions of folklore. A *sui generis* system is a system of its own kind specifically designed to address the needs and concerns of a particular issue. It has been stated that since folklore cannot be successfully accommodated under modern intellectual property concepts, new legal arrangements must be considered to protect the interests of traditional communities in respect of their folklore. An example of a *sui generic* system is the 1982 WIPO/UNESCO 'Model Provisions for National Laws on the Protection of Expressions of

Folklore against Illicit Exploitation and other Prejudicial Actions' (hereinafter the Model Provisions). 'The Model Provisions were developed in response to the concern that expressions of folklore... were susceptible to various forms of illicit exploitation and prejudicial actions', which could prejudice the cultural and economic interests of nations. The Model Provisions have been welcomed as a first step in establishing a *sui generis* system of intellectual property-type protection for expressions of folklore and were seen as a proper guidance for national registration.

The Model Provisions do not define folklore but define expressions of folklore in section 2 as:

> Productions consisting of characteristic elements of the traditional artistic heritage developed and maintained by a community in the country or by individuals reflecting the traditional artistic expectations of such community.

In particular:

(i) Verbal expressions, such as folktales, folk and riddles;

(ii) Musical expressions, such as folk songs and instrumental music;

(iii) Expressions by action, such as folk dances, plays and artistic forms of rituals whether or not reduced to a material form; and

(iv) Tangible expressions such as:

> (a) productions of folk art, in particular drawings, paintings, carvings, sculpture, pottery, terracotta, mosaic, woodwork, metal ware, jewellery, brocket weaving, needlework, textiles, carpets, costumes;

> (b) musical instruments;

> (c) architectural forms.

The terms used in the Model Provisions are 'expressions' and 'productions' as opposed to the term 'works'–this is to underscore the fact that the provisions are *sui generis* rather than part of copyright (Ficsor 1999).

The Model Provisions only cover artistic heritage. This means that traditional beliefs, scientific views or merely practical traditions are not covered under the ambit of the term expressions of folklore. 'Artistic heritage' is given a wide connotation and includes verbal expressions, expressions by action and expressions means of musical sounds.

The Model Provisions state that verbal, musical and expressions by action need not be reduced to any tangible form. This is in recognition of the fact that folkloric expressions often do not have a fixed, material or tangible form, but are still capable of remaining relatively unchanged and well known through the ages.

The Model Provisions protect expressions of folklore from illicit exploitation and from other prejudicial actions. Illicit exploitation is defined in Section 3 as any utilisation made both with gainful intent and outside the traditional or customary context of folklore, without authorisation by a competent authority or the community concerned. This means that any utilisation without gainful intent within the traditional or customary context should not be subject to authorisation. On the other hand any utilisation even by members of the community where the expression has been developed and maintained requires authorisation if it is made outside such context and with gainful intent. Section 3 of the Model Provisions defines use in a traditional context to mean a use where the expression remains in its proper artistic framework based on continuous usage of the community. The same section defines customary usage as utilisation of expressions of folklore in accordance with everyday life of the community.

Section 1 of the Model Provisions provides that certain activities in respect of folklore require authorisation. These activities are publication, reproduction and distribution of copies of expressions of folklore and public recitation, citation, public performance, and transmission by wireless or by wire and any other form of communication to the public.

The Model Provisions allow any member of a community to freely reproduce or perform expressions of folklore of his own community in their traditional or customary context, irrespective of whether it is done with or without gainful intent. In terms of section 4 of the Model Provisions there is no need to obtain authorisation for the utilisation of an expression of folklore where the use is for an educational purpose; or if the expression of folklore is by way of illustration in an original work; or the work is borrowed for creating an original work by the author and comprises incidental utilisation. The Model Provisions in section 6 provide penal sanctions for certain actions deemed detrimental to interests related to the use of the expressions of folklore. These are:

- The failure to indicate the source of the expression of folklore by mentioning the community and/or geographic place from where the expression utilised has been derived;

- Unauthorised utilisation of an expression of folklore where authorisation is required constitutes an offence;

- Using an expression without authorisation is also constituted by uses going beyond the limits or which are contrary to the conditions of an authorisation obtained.

- Any public utilisation distorting the expression of folklore, in any direct or indirect manner, which is prejudicial to the cultural interests, is an offence.

All four offences require wilful intent on the part of the offender. However, as regards the issue of non-compliance with the requirement of acknowledgment of source and the need to obtain authorisation to use the expression of folklore, the Model Provisions also allow for punishment of acts committed negligently.

The Model Provisions can be adopted as a separate law, as a chapter in IPR law, or as a decree or decree law, which does not necessarily constitute a statute.

The Model Provisions are however limited in a number of ways. They only protect artistic heritage and not the entire cultural heritage of a nation. They are therefore inadequate to provide protection to the vital elements of folklore. It has been argued that 'the arena [of the Model Provisions] needs to be enlarged so as to cover a wide spectrum of creative indigenous collections belonging to the community' (Valsala 2002).

This section has discussed the alternative regimes for the protection of folklore and traditional knowledge. They are by no means perfect but can be used to supplement or to complement the conventional intellectual property regimes where they are lacking.

Conclusion

Contemporary intellectual property regimes do not adequately protect folklore. The difficulty of trying to protect folklore as intellectual property arises from the fact that intellectual property espouses tenets of individualism and economic value which tenets are not embraced by indigenous owners of folklore. Folklore is created, owned and utilised differently from conventional intellectual property rights. Folklore, unlike intellectual property, is designed not to confer economic benefits on individual creators but is intended to be exploited communally by the community which owns it. Attempts to protect folklore by intellectual property rights are also complicated by the inherent requirements of intellectual property protection such as originality, novelty, industrial application and the limited term of protection. It is submitted therefore that folklore aspects which can be protected by intellectual property should be so protected but other measures must also be used to complement and supplement the intellectual prorate system. It is further submitted that developing countries should seek to enact *sui generis* intellectual property systems to protect their folklore and to complement these with other mechanisms such as documentation. These *sui generis* regimes must be specifically adapted to the nature of folklore, to ensure effective protection. These regimes must take what is effective in the intellectual property system and combine it with other forms of protection to try and achieve protection of folklore.

References

Asein, J., 1998, 'Intellectual Property Rights for New Beneficiaries; Folklore and Intellectual Property', Paper presented at the WIPO Regional Colloquium on the Teaching of Intellectual Property Law, Pretoria, 12-15 October, 1998.

Daes, E.A, 1993, 'Discrimination Against Indigenous Peoples: Study on the Protection of Cultural and Intellectual in Puri', *Intellectual Property Journal*, Vol. 7.

Daes, E.A., 1995, 'Cultural ownership and intellectual property rights Post-Mabo: Putting Ideas into Action', *Intellectual Property Journal*, Vol. 9, p. 293.

Ficsor. M., 1999, 'Indigenous Peoples and Local Communities: Exploration of Issues Related to Intellectual Property Protection of Expressions of Traditional Culture ('Expressions of Folklore')', Paper Presented at International Association for the Advancement of Teaching and Research in Intellectual Property, Geneva, Switzerland, 7-9 July 1999.

Janke, T., 2002, 'Minding Culture: Case Studies on Intellectual Property and Traditional Expressions', at http://www.wipo.int/tk/en/studies/cultural/minding-culture/studies/ index. html.

Mugabe, J., 1998, 'Intellectual Property and Traditional Knowledge', in WIPO, 1999, Intellectual Property and Human Rights, WIPO publication No. 762 (E).

Oman, R., 1997, 'Folkloric Treasures: The Next Copyright Frontier?', *IPL Newsletter*, Vol 15, No. 4, p.3.

Posey, et al., 1993, 'Indigenous Peoples, Biotechnology and Intellectual Property Rights', 2, *Review of European Community and International Environmental Law*, p.141.

Thebe, S.T., 1999, 'Protecting Traditional Medical Knowledge as Intellectual Property', *Lesotho Law Journal*, Vol. 12, No. 2, pp.74-93.

Kutty Valsala G., 2002, 'A Study on the Protection of Expressions of Folklore', at http//www.wipo.Int/tkl/en/studies/cultural/expressions/study/kutty.pdf.

WIPO, 1998a, *Intellectual Property Reading Material*, Second edition, WIPO Publication No. 476 (E).

WIPO, 1998b, *Intellectual Property in Asia and the Pacific*, January-June, WIPO Publication No. 435 (E).

WIPO, 2001, *Report on Fact Finding Mission on the Intellectual Property Needs and Expectations of Traditional Knowledge Holders* (1998-99), WIPO Publication No. 768 (E).

WIPO, 2003, 'Consolidated analysis of the legal protection of traditional cultural expressions', available at http//www.wipo.int/documents/en/meetings/2003/igc/doc/grtkf-1c-5-3. doc.

5

Copyright in the Digital Era and Some Implications for Indigenous Knowledge

Kgomotso H. Moahi

What Is Copyright?

Copyright is a concept that is not generally understood. According to Litman (quoted in Samuelson, 2002), this is ironic considering that it applies to the everyday things that people do, for example, recording music for their own personal use and photocopying documents. People are blissfully unaware of what copyright entails and means to them, both as creators and users of knowledge.

Copyright represents one aspect of intellectual property rights (IP). IP rights are meant to reward, recognise and encourage innovation and creativity. They bestow upon the recipients the right to profit from their innovation, and the right to contest against anyone who appropriates their rights. Examples of IP include the granting of copyrights, patents, trademarks and trade names.

Strong (1994) has simply described copyright as a limited monopoly granted to the author in order to provide the financial incentive for people to create works of literature, art, etc. A definition of copyright from the World Intellectual Property Organisation (WIPO) document on intellectual property reads as follows:

> When a person creates a literary, musical, scientific or artistic work, he or she is the owner of that work and is free to decide on its use. That person (called the 'creator' or the 'author' or 'owner of rights') can control the destiny of the work... Copyright is the legal protection extended to the

owner of the rights in an original work that he has created. It comprises two main sets of rights: the economic rights and the moral rights (WIPO, 2003). Economic rights refer to the rights that the owners of the work have to making a profit from their work - 'The rights of reproduction, broadcasting, public performance, adaptation, translation, and public recitation, public display, distribution and so on'. Moral rights refer to the right of the author to have his/her name prominently indicated on the work and to object to any use of that work that he/she deems to be a distortion, mutilation or any other modification.

Copyright protects the intellectual rights of authors and thus encourages them to continue contributing to knowledge. Mears (2003) notes that: 'The purpose of copyright is to promote the progress of science and useful arts and to encourage others to build freely upon the ideas and information conveyed in a work'. The idea is that authors are encouraged to produce more knowledge by being given the rights to benefit commercially and otherwise from their work. Potential authors are also encouraged through guidelines known as 'fair use' to build upon the ideas of others and produce even more knowledge. Thus, copyright aims at 'creating a conducive environment to entice the human mind to create and invest' (*Botswana Guardian*, 2003). Copyright encourages people to be creative since they get to control and even benefit from their creativity. It also encourages others to generate new knowledge by enabling them to use the ideas of others as long as certain conditions are met.

The main international agreement on copyright is the Berne Convention of 1886, administered by the World Intellectual Property Organisation (WIPO). In addition, most countries have fashioned their own copyright laws. WIPO is an international organisation tasked with promoting the intellectual property of works. It is a UN specialised agency based in Geneva and has a country membership of 179. It administers a total of 23 treaties dealing with different aspects of intellectual property. One of these treaties is the Berne Convention of 1886 that has been revised several times over the years in relation to the impact that technology has on copyright laws and the protection that could be accorded to the authors and creators as a result. The Convention was signed to protect the rights of authors of literary and artistic works, and all member countries that have ratified the Convention are bound by its provisions. The Berne Convention stipulates that copyright usually lasts for the life of the author, plus an additional 50 years. After that the work is then in the 'public domain'- i.e., it can be used without the author's permission because copyright has expired. Copyright is assumed as soon as works have been put down in a fixed format - there is no need to follow a formal application process.

The Doctrine of Fair Use

The fair use doctrine consists of a set of guidelines that outline what constitutes allowable use of copyrighted material. The fair use doctrine enables or encourages the development and progress of knowledge by making copyright flexible enough to allow copyright materials to be the basis of new knowledge. There are four criteria used to judge whether the use of copyright protected materials constitute fair use or not. These criteria have been used by various courts, especially in the US, to evaluate whether there has been an infringement of copyright. The criteria follow below:

(i) The purpose and character of use, that is, whether the work is used for educational purposes, and research. If the material has been used for other purposes, for example, for commercial gain, then copyright has been infringed;

(ii) The factual or creative nature of the original work - this means that when the copyrighted material has been used to produce a non-fiction work, then the individual gets more points for fair use than someone who has produced a fictional work;

(iii) The amount and substantive value of the work being copied relative to the work as a whole. Reproducing a large portion of the works, such as the whole book or more than a third of it is regarded as infringement of copyright;

(iv) The effect that the use of the work has on the market value of the copyrighted work, that is whether the use of a copyrighted work has affected the economic gains of that work owing to the creator.

The rule is that if a work is used to create a new work, what is called transformative use, this constitutes what is called fair use. However, if it is just a direct copy, with no transformative value then this is definitely copyright infringement. In addition, if that work is copied in order to gain commercially from it, then copyright has been infringed.

Thus we see that the fair use rule is an exception of the copyright laws, where materials can be reproduced without first seeking the author's permission. This applies when the use of the material is not for financial gain, but is used for educational purposes or informing the public. This is why scholars are able to reproduce freely materials from journals and books and to also quote from other sources, as long as they do not do it for financial gain, but for education and research purposes.

Use is considered not to be fair where the use of a work may affect the returns of the materials in terms of sales. For example, this is the case when by photocopying or recording an item you prevent potential buyers from going out to purchase the item. This obviously affects even libraries whose lending of books may be considered to be harming the potential returns of the authors. Fair use, especially in the US, has been built up through case law over the years.

Copyright and Fair Use in the Digital Era

There is no doubt that ICTs have changed intellectual property rights as they have affected many other things. Concerns of copyright in the digital world were first raised in the US, subsequent to the formation of President Clinton's Information Infrastructure Task Force (IITF). The IITF was tasked with articulating the administration's vision of a National Information Infrastructure (NII). The issue became the mandate of the Working Group on Intellectual Property Rights. The Working Group considered that a conference on fair use in the digital era (CONFU), bringing together copyright holders and educationalists and interested parties, was required to try and develop guidelines for fair use in the digital era. The working group met many times and developed guidelines, although they failed to reach consensus on the applicability of these guidelines. In the absence of anything else guiding fair use in the digital environment, many institutions and universities, especially in the US, have adopted the guidelines. These guidelines refer to a number of circumstances when digital copying might need to be carried out. For example it covers the digitization of images for use in teaching and scholarly work. It is permissible for educators to digitize analogue images as long as they use thumbnail sketches of those images (small scale, usually low resolution digital representations of the image). Educators may also use images for teaching and scholarly presentations, but would be required to seek permission if they were to be published. Multimedia works may be created for either teaching or for scholarly presentations, but with limitations on the amount of text, music, lyrics, video clips, etc that may be included in the presentation. The multimedia work may only be used for a period of two years only.

As can be seen, fair use makes it possible for individuals to make reference to other people's ideas and reproduce them, provided it is for academic study, for example, carrying out research or used for teaching purposes. However, this works very well (or fairly well) when the material is in printed format - for example, books and periodical articles. Copyright enforcement in the printed environment by nature is difficult on many fronts. First, creators and authors have the right to prohibit or bring forth a case if they perceive that their rights have been infringed. However, the monitoring required in this case is practically impossible for them. Hence, we see the existence of collective copyright management organisations which look after the interests of creators and authors in many countries. Secondly, even though the restrictions on the use of materials are set out in the copyright laws, interpretation of these has been subject to a lot of debate and law-suits in the US.

The advent of the Internet or the web has had a number of implications for both publishers and users: it is easy to publish information and that information becomes instantly available to thousands of people all over the world. This is an advantage for publishers/creators because it has lowered the cost of distribution after the initial production. However, this has created a problem for both publishers/owners and the users of information. On the one hand, for publishers/owners, the easy distribution and availability of materials on the Internet meant that the economic returns (i.e., from sales) of the works would be severely curtailed because once the material is available digitally, distribution becomes easy. On the other hand, for users the concerns of the owners meant that publishers/owners would want to take measures to curtail access to information as is being done now through licensing. This is the dilemma currently facing copyright in the digital era.

The economics of information have also been altered somewhat by the digital era (Samuelson 2002). Digital information has changed the economics of reproduction, because making copies of works has become very easy, the cost has gone down, and the quality is very good. In the digital world, opportunities for theft are much greater than they were before (Strong 1994). In addition, the electronic media, namely the Internet, makes it so easy for individuals to make perfect copies of materials to the extent that it is not possible for one to easily recognise a copy. Thus a piece of work can be distributed and circulated by individuals other than the owners/publishers, as well as altered, and no-one being the wiser for it.

Materials that are available on the Internet are regarded as being in a fixed, tangible medium (Stanford University 2003) because they are stored somewhere in some file server. This means therefore that such work is subject to copyright, and therefore, should not be copied *verbatim*. One should note though, that the very use of digital material involves copying or downloading the materials in order to read them. This means that the very use of digital materials is in itself an infringement of copyright because the basic fundamental concept underlying copyright is the copying of materials. There is an inherent contradiction that seemingly renders the concept of copyright in the digital era untenable. This is an issue that has not been resolved as some people believe that downloading is legal and others believe that it is not (Mears 2003). It is from this dilemma that online publishers have opted for the licensing of materials, so that only those with the permission may download materials in order to use them. In some instances, publishers have used technology to disable the downloading, and therefore access to their materials. All of this challenges the intent of copyright, which is not only to protect the rights of the creators, but to also make it possible for the public to access materials in order for them to be able to create more from the espoused ideas and notions.

Networks have changed the economics of distribution—once a work is put on the Internet, it becomes instantaneously available to millions of people. It is therefore easy for publishers to distribute their work, and also easy for the public to distribute unauthorised works, such as pirate copies of movies and music, beta versions of software, and manuscripts that are not yet published. The easy distribution of information has meant that publishers and owners prefer to license rather than sell their works to users in the digital media. Again this action has given more rights to authors and publishers - thus tipping the delicate balance that copyright is attempting to strike.

In the print era, copyright was about how other people's works were used. But according to Pike (2002), the tendency in the digital environment has become to control access since use is very difficult to police. This has upset the 'first sale' doctrine as found in the printed information era. First sale meant that individuals and libraries could, once they had bought a book, be able to lend it out or re-sell it at second hand book sales, etc. Licensing on the other hand, means that the licensee has limited transfer of rights of use with stated conditions and terms. It means that the works are not the property of the licensee, to use even years later once the license has elapsed. In a sense, the licensee (for example, an individual or a library), is tied to the provider for as long as they need the material. This also affects the archiving of material for posterity. Libraries are about storing knowledge for posterity, in the digital environment where materials are licensed, this mandate is difficult to fulfil for libraries.

Digitized data can be easily manipulated and modified. Whilst it was not an easy matter to determine what was fair use of materials in the print world (as evidenced by law suits in order to rule on what was fair use or not), it has become extremely difficult in the digitized, electronic era. This is so because users are now able to obtain data freely from the Internet and other networked sources and are able to create new works by culling from different sources and the restriction on copyright is just not evident in this environment. This has enabled the creation of multimedia documents. Putting together a multimedia document means putting together different types of data obtained from different sources. For example, if preparing a presentation on the Bee Gees, a student/author might want to include video clips, sound clips, etc., to illustrate their point. This means that issues to do with copyright are extremely difficult because of the myriad of sources that might be used.

An important point is that the moral and economic rights of authors and creators are seriously under threat. With the commercial development of the Internet, publishing conglomerates have taken over the copyrights of authors who then no longer have a say as to what happens to their creations. The fact that materials can be easily copied and distributed puts the rights of authors and creators in serious jeopardy.

Intellectual Property Rights and Indigenous Knowledge

Indigenous knowledge (IK) can be defined as a body of knowledge belonging to communities or ethnic groups, shaped by their culture, traditions and way of life. The term is sometimes used interchangeably with traditional knowledge. IK is home-grown knowledge that enables communities to make sense of who they are and to interact with their environment in ways that sustain life. It is knowledge that arises from life experience, and which is passed down from generation to generation through word of mouth in the form of folklore, idioms, proverbs, songs, rites of passage and rituals. IK covers the broad spectrum of life, and therefore there are different types of IK, ranging from people's beliefs, medicine, to arts and crafts, etc. While knowledge in general is described as being explicit and tacit, IK is mainly tacit as it resides in people heads, and has for the most part, not being codified. Indigenous knowledge has a number of unique characteristics:

(a) Any one single individual does not own IK because it is a product of the culture tradition and way of life of a community. It is thus community owned;

(b) It is usually passed orally from generation to generation, it is not codified or documented anywhere except in the minds of the community and the community's knowledge custodians, such as chiefs, traditional doctors, etc.;

(c) It has a potential (and has in many cases) to provide economic returns either to the community that owns it, or to the individuals who may have taken it away from the community for meagre economic gain, or through some other fraudulent means. It is thus a very valuable resource, and this has prompted more debate on the intellectual property rights of IK.

There has been recognition of the economic potential of IK over the past few years, and this has brought issues of intellectual rights of IK to the fore. It is very clear that IK has contributed significantly to some medicinal and cosmetic products in use today. But it was not until 1992 that the importance of IK was recognised and the Convention of Biological Diversity (CBD) was put in place. There is however, a contradiction between intellectual property and indigenous knowledge. Intellectual property, according to Blakeney (1999), represents the 'propertisation' of traditional knowledge, and by definition traditional knowledge is not individual property. IK is generally perceived to be a collective property and is owned by communities. However such communities are usually not able to take control of this knowledge and this often becomes the responsibility of custodians such as chiefs. It has historically been the case that these chiefs have 'sold' IK without due consideration for the long-term implications of this on their communities.

Patenting is a way of protecting intellectual property that goes some way in assigning intellectual property rights. An example is the granting of a patent for the *Hoodia* cactus to the San community in South Africa (Mutula 2002). The problem though for most other communities is that they have limited legal know how and are unable to engage agents of multinationals who appropriate their IK for their own gains. Where they can negotiate for their rights, the struggle has been protracted. The experience of the San people in securing recognition of ownership, and a share of the profits from the Hoodia cactus patent, is a case in point that illustrates the difficulties that communities will have in claiming their rights. The San sued South Africa's Council for Scientific and Industrial Research in 2000 for patenting the properties of Hoodia, which, they claimed was their IK. Negotiations took three years, and were only concluded in March 2003. The question is: how many communities have the wherewithal and tenacity to engage an organisation as big as the National Research Council?

However, because IK is not documented, there is a danger that it will disappear as people steeped in the ways and knowledge of communities die off. This is a very real danger because as more people become educated, they come to think that only knowledge that has been through the rigors of scientific, laboratory experimentation is real knowledge. They tend to view IK as being inferior and based on hunches and superstitions. There is therefore a need to preserve this information and knowledge, as it is in fact valuable to society. Preserving it however means documenting it. Once a work is documented in a fixed format, it is automatically copyrighted. The question here is who owns the copyright - is it the community from which it was obtained, or is it the individual or organisation that took the responsibility to document the knowledge? Ideally, the community should have the controlling rights, but practically this has not always been the case. Historians and anthropologists have studied communities and recorded their culture, traditions, way of life and indigenous knowledge, and have claimed the credit. Pharmaceutical companies and cosmetic companies have used plants and extracts that are known to local communities as being beneficial in one way or the other and have appropriated that technology in most cases in return for a pittance compared to the profits that they have made.

In many developing countries, such as Botswana, legislation for intellectual property rights has not really been enforced, because it was not regarded as a priority after independence (*Botswana Guardian* 2003). There is generally very little, if any, protection for traditional knowledge holders in Botswana, hence there have been instances of intellectual property infringement that were recently published in the media, such as the Hoodia cactus stories.

Indigenous knowledge property rights are generally included in the branch of intellectual property known as industrial property. However, IK property rights are still very much under discussion locally and internationally. Even the World Intellectual Property Organisation has not yet been able to promulgate the regulations for intellectual property for traditional or indigenous knowledge holders. However, some progress has been made with the establishment of working bodies within WIPO to establish ways and means of protecting traditional indigenous knowledge. The Berne Convention on Copyright and the Agreement on Trade Related Aspects of Intellectual Property Rights (TRIPS) are some agreements that attempt to protect IK from abuse and piracy. However, according to Raseroka (2002), these instruments are oriented more towards the modern knowledge systems rather than to IK and therefore are inadequate in protecting the rights of communities where their IK is concerned. The intellectual property regimes have been found wanting in protecting indigenous knowledge. This is due to the contradictions between the basic tenets of copyright: ownership and authorship; material form; originality; duration; and rights in derivative works (Githaiga 1998) on the one hand, and the nature of IK on the one hand. As noted above, copyright gives individuals the right to knowledge that they have created. IK is not individually owned, but belongs to the entire community. Under copyright, works have to be original creations. IK is mostly inspired and derived from previous eras and built upon and developed with time. Accordingly, the concept of originality does not resonate with IK, which for the most part is oral knowledge passed that way from generation to generation. For copyright purposes, IK must be represented in a fixed form, i.e., written down. Copyright subsists during the lifetime of the author and for another fifty years after his death. IK is timeless; it is a product of many lifetimes that has been carried over many generations.

Digitizing Indigenous Knowledge

More and more indigenous and cultural heritage is being digitized. According to Britz and Lor (2003), there have been quite a few projects in Africa where IK has been digitized. There are a number of activities and initiatives aimed at capturing Africa's IK, one of which is the World Bank IK Programme which maintains a database of IK, where people and communities can contribute. Whilst this may be a positive development that enables people who would not otherwise know or come to appreciate other people's culture to do so, it also poses a number of moral questions (Britz and Lor 2003). Britz and Lor pose the following question: 'will the originating communities be identified as the original creators of their cultural heritage and will they have the right to control access and non-disclosure of certain categories of their cultural heritage, for example, sacred knowledge artefacts' (Britz and Lor 2003: 4). The WIPO Intergovernmental Committee on Intellectual Property and Genetic Resources, Traditional Knowledge and Folklore (IGC) set up in 2000 still does not have the answers to these questions. Of concern to IK holders is the right to be acknowledged and to prevent derogatory, offensive and fallacious use of their heritage (WIPO 2003).

In general intellectual property rights for IK are needed for the following reasons (Anon.):

(i) The right to own and control one's own knowledge;

(ii) The right to prevent and control commercial use of that knowledge;

(iii) The right to benefit commercially;

(iv) The right to be acknowledged and attributed to the knowledge; and

(v) The right to prevent derogatory, offensive and fallacious use of the knowledge.

IK generally belongs to communities, and once such knowledge is digitized, then one may wonder whether the communities from which it originates will have rights to it, and if so what sort of rights, given the general powerlessness of communities against multinationals. Will they be able to exercise the rights outlined above? History has shown otherwise. Communities have been unable to control their rights once their knowledge has been codified or digitized; they have been powerless to prevent their knowledge from being commercialised and used in derogatory ways.

Britz and Lor (2003) have proposed a number of broad principles that should guide the digitization of indigenous knowledge, and which the present author feels could be extended to copyright issues of indigenous knowledge in the digital era. Digitization should not lead to trivialisation of the culture where it is used, and for enriching other people other than the community who owns the IK. Communities should own the IK and have a say in what should or should not be digitized. IK owners should maintain their ownership rights. The IK ownership should not fall into the hands of those digitizing it – as it did in the past with those who were documenting it.

Conclusion

The concept of copyright as we know it is being challenged by the digitization of information and the proliferation of networks, in particular, the Internet. Many concepts enshrined in copyright, such as fair use and first sale doctrine, are under siege. Copyright has moved from being a concern of publishers and writers only, because the very essence of copyright (copying/downloading) is at the heart of using the technology that many people in the world now have access to. With issues of copyright being unclear in the digital environment, and the concern for developing nations to put content into the Internet, there are more questions than answers on the copyright of indigenous and cultural heritage in the digital environment.

Many developing countries' intellectual property laws have vestiges of their former colonisers' thinking embodied in them. Many of these countries, such as Botswana, are in the process of developing new copyright laws, with the assistance of WIPO. There is a need therefore for these countries to take note of some of the issues that arise from copyright and the electronic environment. All scenarios must be legislated for to avoid ambiguity. What should be made very clear is that the answer by commercial content producers to the copyright issue has been the use of protective software (encryption, fingerprinting, digital signatures, licensing, etc). This however, does not bode well for developing countries that lack the resources to purchase access to information. Given the fact that access to information is a human right, governments and civil society in developing countries need to ensure that most of content that they place on the Internet is accessible to their populations, and contains very clearly stipulated copyright notices.

Even as WIPO through the Intergovernmental Committee on Genetic Resources, Traditional Knowledge and Folklore is still working out approaches to protect indigenous knowledge, there is also a need for governments and civil society in developing countries to think very carefully about what needs to be done to safeguard the intellectual property of communities that own IK. One idea is that countries should develop IK databases that would indicate what IK there is, who or which community owns it, etc. The idea here would be that such a database could be used to check whenever individuals are claiming or applying for IP rights. When IK is being digitized, a clear statement of IP should be included that shows who the owner(s) are, and under what conditions the IK could be used – something similar to the license notices that are displayed when one uses computer software.

References

Blakeney, Michael, 1999, 'IP in the Dreamtime – Protecting the Cultural Creativity of

Indigenous Peoples', *Oxford IP Research Centre Research Seminar*, 9 November, at: http://www.oiprc.ox.ac.uk/EJWP1199.html. Accessed on 9/12/2003.

Botswana Government Gazette, 2000, *Copyright and Neighbouring Rights Act 2000*.

Johannes Britz and Peter Lor, 2003, 'A Moral Reflection on the Digitization of Africa's Documentary Heritage', *World Library and Information Congress*, 69th IFLA General Conference and Council. 1-9 August 2003, Berlin.

Educom Review Staff, Educom Review, 'Copyright and Fair Use in the Digital Age: Q&A with Peter Lyman', at: Http://www.educase.edu/pub/er/review/reviewaerticles/30132.html: accessed on 31/10/2003.

Githaiga, Joseph, 1998, 'IP Law and the Protection of Indigenous Folklore and Knowledge', at: http://www.murdoch.edu.au/. Accessed on: 8/12/2003.

Litman, Jessica, 2001, *Digital Copyright*, Amherst, New York, Prometheus Books.

Mears, Garret, 2003, 'Copyright in the Information Age', at: http://filebox.vt.edu/users/gmears/internet/gmears_paper.html Accessed on: 9/08/2003.

Mutula, Stephen, 2002, 'The Digital Divide in Sub-Saharan Africa: Implications for the Revitalization and Preservation of Indigenous Knowledge Systems', in *SCECSAL 2002: From Africa to the world - the globalization of indigenous knowledge systems*, 15-19 April 2002, South Africa, pp 119-141.

Pike, George H., 2002, 'The Delicate Dance of Database Licenses, Copyright, and Fair Use', *Computers in Libraries*, Vol. 22, No. 5, May.

Raseroka, H. Kay, 2002, 'From Africa to the World - the Globalization of Indigenous Knowledge Systems: setting the scene', Keynote address, SCECSAL 2002, *From Africa to the world- the globalization of indigenous knowledge systems*, 15-19 April, South Africa, pp.1-12.

Samuelson. Pamela, 2000, 'The Digital Dilemma: A Perspective on Intellectual Property in the Information Age', Paper presented at the 28th Annual Telecommunications Policy Research Conference.

Samuelson, Pamela, 2002, 'Towards a "New Deal" for Copyright for and Information Age', 100, *Michigan Law Review*.

Stanford University Libraries, Copyright and Fair Use, at: http://fairuse.Stanford.edu/Copyright_and_Fair_Use_Overview/chapter0/9-a.html Accessed on 1/9/2003.

Strong, William S., 1994, 'Copyright in the New World of Electronic Publishing', Presented at the Workshop 'Electronic Publishing Issues II', Association of American Universities Presses Annual Meeting, 17 June, Washington, DC.

WIPO, 'Intellectual Property and Genetic Resources, Traditional Knowledge and Folklore', at: http//www.wipo.org/about-ip/en/publications/genetic_resources.htm. Accessed on 23/10/2003.

WIPO, 'What rights does copyright provide?', at: http://www.wipo.org/about-ip/en/about_copyright.html Accessed on: 23/10/2003.

WIPO, 'Collective Management of Copyright and related rights', at: http://www.wipo.org/about-ip/en/about_collective_mngt.html Accessed on: 23/10/2003.

6

The Gods Are Resting There: Challenges to the Protection of Heritage Sites through Legislation and Local Knowledge

Alinah K. Segobye

Introduction

Heritage is, simply defined, anything which is transmitted from ancestors or past ages (Chambers 1990). It is also defined as 'our legacy from the past, what we live today, and what we pass on to future generations' (UNESCO 1998). To most people, heritage is strongly linked to how they express their identity, culture and history. It is their conception of the aesthetic or significant. It principally includes human-made objects within the landscape but most cultures would also include natural places which are valued for their religious or sacred significance. Heritage management as a profession can be seen as emerging mainly within Europe and America in the post-Second World War period with the professionalisation of practice and the development of international codes. It is clear that heritage management is principally articulated through legal codes which govern the treatment of heritage resources. In this regard, Europe is a pace-setter in the enactment of heritage protection legislation. The earliest recorded efforts date to 1666 when the Swedish Crown declared protection of all Swedish heritage resources. Other European countries followed in the nineteenth century with legislation principally aimed at protecting heritage resources particularly archaeological heritage from plunder and destruction. In its modern practice, heritage resources management and its related sub-discipline archaeological heritage management were formally developed in the 1960s with the growth of New Archaeology and a conscious desire to protect the environment from the rapid development within countries globally (Cleere 1989).

The concept of heritage is controversial and what constitutes heritage is often contentious (Ascherson 2000). This is mainly because 'a Eurocentric legacy dominates models of valuing the past throughout the world, even among people long deprived by, or at odds with, Europeanization' (Lowenthal 1990: 302). Further, the past provides contemporary societies with the means of reinforcing or confirming their identities which may be in conflict. As a result, heritage is selective in its representation of the past. Lowenthal further notes that:

> Relics remain essential bridges between then and now. They confirm or deny what we think of it, symbolize or memorialize communal links over time, and provide archaeological metaphors that illumine the process of history and memory (Lowenthal 1985: xxiii).

In Africa, heritage combines both cultural (human-made objects and materials in the landscape) and natural places used both in the past and present as sacred, religious or otherwise significant places. Heritage includes also the intangible things such as ideas, or knowledge systems held and passed on in an oral medium from generation to generation (Pressouyre 1995). The Euro-American notion of heritage has often focussed mainly on tangible material remains as recorded through archaeological research and on the use of classical definitions of antiquities and relics as artefacts. These definitions ignored the fact that other cultures had knowledge systems which accorded protection to heritage resources and bestowed meaning to these places which could only be understood through specific cultural media and contexts.

As a profession, heritage management has drawn mainly from the discipline of archaeology for its methodologies. These rely mainly in the identification of sites, relics or monuments, and an ascription of value based on their presumed scientific or other significance. Archaeologists mainly determined value on the basis of the potential scientific value of objects and their contribution to knowledge. As a result, many heritage sites were declared on the basis of their scientific value with very little inputs from the communities within which they were found. Over the last two decades however, the practice of archaeology has changed significantly. This move followed the formation of the World Archaeological Congress which advocated the inclusion of other archaeologies, particularly indigenous minorities, in the practice of archaeology. Archaeology thus lodged itself in the present within the landscapes of social, political and other discourses of the past. This change in archaeology was also manifested in new concerns within heritage management with changes in legislation and professional practice to incorporate the views of local communities. Public archaeology was thus an effort to engender 'the position of human rights in archaeology, and in particular, the rights of indigenous populations to take or at least to share in decisions on the treatment, interpretation and management of their sites and material relics' (Ascherson 2000: 2-3).

Heritage managers, in the main, claim to exercise their professions as custodians of public property. In practice, the state or other state-related agencies often hold the ownership rights of heritage resources. The public, for whom the property is held, often have very little inputs into the drafting of legislation governing access to heritage resources, their use or benefits accruing from them. In Southern Africa, the legacy of colonialism has often meant that legislation enacted to protect heritage was based principally on European law. As a result, legislation in many of the Southern African countries reflects European definitions of heritage. Citing Turnbridge and Ashworth (1996), Manyanga (2000) notes that the colonial period brought into conflict European and African heritages with the resultant domination of African heritage by Europe. The end of the colonial era therefore rendered as irrelevant colonial heritage and attempts to reclaim African heritage by post-colonial states in nation-building exercises. However, given the legislation also inherited by new governments, it was inevitable that the colonial heritage remained protected thus becoming a burden for indigenous societies. From another viewpoint, Cleere argues that:

> The end of colonialism... and the birth of new nations have seen the promotion of archaeological heritage management in a more positive sense... Colonialism created a discontinuity in many of these [African] countries, which is being counteracted by the use of monuments to demonstrate a continuous cultural identity within which the colonial period was no more than an irrelevant episode (Cleere 1989: 8).

Heritage, therefore, remained a challenge for heritage managers, particularly in post-colonial Southern Africa where choices of what to preserve, conserve or represent were not clear cut and were heavily influenced by past legacies and contemporary desires to forge new identities within emergent nation states. The discussion below will highlight this dilemma using Botswana as an example.

2. The Evolution of Heritage Legislation in Botswana

The current national legislation for the protection of heritage in Botswana originates in the 1930s with the Bushman Relics Proclamation (68 of 1934). This Proclamation bestowed protection on archaeological sites which had become vulnerable to looters and antiquarian collectors who were active in the then Southern Rhodesia and South Africa. Lists of gazetted national monuments were then initiated and were added to over the next three decades until the Act was revised and promulgated as the Monuments and Relics Act 1970 (Campbell 1998: 30). This Act has subsequently been revised (2001) and is in operation today. Other related pieces of legislation are the Anthropological Research Act 1967 (Cap 59:02) which deals with the protection of communities and their knowledge systems, and the Cinematograph Act 1972 (Cap 60:02) which deals with the production of films and other media. Like the Anthropological Research Act, the latter Act is overdue for revision but in its intent accords some protection to communities and their knowledge systems. Unfortunately the lack of enforcement resources has, over time, meant that the two Acts have been violated and communities have been objectified in research and cultural media production without due protection for their knowledge systems or ethical treatment of their cultural heritage.

The Monuments and Relics Act 2001 provides for several categories of heritage resources such as ancient monument, ancient working, historic buildings, protected heritage areas, sites, relics and recent artefacts, to list some. These categories essentially identify types of material objects recognised for purposes of bestowing protection. An important provision of the Act is the definition of an 'ancient monument' as:

> Any building, ruin, remaining portion of a building or ruin, ancient working, stone circle, grave, cave, rock shelter, midden, mound, archaeological site, or other site or thing of a similar kind, which is known or believed to have been erected, constructed or used in Botswana before 1st June 1902' (Botswana Government 2001).

In principle, this should cover a diverse range of places and objects made and used by Batswana in the past. In practice however, the law accords selective representation to objects in that in the main it is objects of archaeological significance or colonial origin which receive this protection, whilst indigenous or traditional heritage objects such as traditional architecture and material culture do not receive it or suffer attrition as a direct result of modernisation. This is particularly evident in the loss of knowledge in the area of traditional architecture and decor.

The National Museum is the custodian authority for the Monuments and Relics Act and through its various departments is responsible for ensuring the development and protection of sites in the landscape. From archaeological research in Botswana, it is quite clear that the resources at the disposal of the National Museum and the regional community museums are insufficient for this task. While a few sites and gazetted national monuments gain protection such as fencing, erection of sign-posts and sometimes the deployment of custodians at the sites, most of the sites are left to the challenges of nature. They undergo tremendous site transformation processes, particularly sites with stone walls which are regularly destroyed by people and animals. More recently the acceleration of development projects such as roads and the provision of water resources to rural areas have resulted in the unprecedented destruction of heritage sites. Even though these sites may be subjected to Environmental Impact Assessment Studies (EIAs), most are still destroyed in the course of development projects.

The approach of heritage protection adopted by the National Museum in accordance with the provisions of the Act also poses a challenge to the nature of protection accorded to the sites. Unfortunately, because the Act often recognises sites as entities defined by particular attributes, the delimitation of sites gazetted for protection often ignores wider landscapes within which the sites are located, often resulting in the creation of barriers between parts of sites and others which communities could be using for other purposes. Further, the co-existence of archaeological or cultural heritage sites within the context of National Parks which are governed by the National Parks and Game Reserves Regulations 2000 often brings into conflict the interests of communities in accessing heritage resources which they would traditionally have used as part of their livelihoods and construction of their world views.

Another interesting dimension in the protection of heritage sites is the role of the National Museum as the authority responsible for the issuance of research permits for archaeological research. The Museum periodically undertakes its own research. Archaeological research is, by its very nature, destructive. In recent times it has become apparent that some communities have come to associate excavations in their landscapes as a source of negative power (karma). An example can be drawn in the protests of communities at recent excavations at Bosutswe Hill in the central district. Local prophets blamed the death of members of their churches and indeed people in the communities in the neighbouring areas on the work of archaeologists excavating at Bosutswe (Denbow pers. comm. 2002; 2003). What emerged from this case is that where archaeological excavations have, in the past, not been perceived as threatening to the well being of communities, the advent of high mortality rates in the era of HIV/AIDS in the country served to reinforce people's fears that supernatural forces or *Badimo* had been angered by activities of those who 'disturb' them in their resting places.

Other reactions of communities to perceived disturbances of their *Badimo* by archaeologists and other development workers arose during attempts to develop a dam on the Lotsane River in the vicinity of the Tswapong Hills.

The Batswapong, legendary for their strong beliefs in the power of *Badimo* and their residence in the Tswapong Hills have, over time, woven a powerful belief system blending nature and culture which serves as the anchor of Tswapong identity. Previous attempts to develop infrastructure in the Hills have been rejected by the communities in the area, and the attempt to develop a dam cutting off communities' access to the Hills sparked a number of debates and protracted negotiations between the developing authority, namely the Department of Water Affairs, and communities in the area. What this example highlighted was the manner in which community knowledge and belief systems could impact on development projects unless their full support has been solicited and they are assisted to interpret and internalise the significance of proposed changes within their heritage spaces. Happily, the spirit of *kgotla* which guided the project resulted in a number of strategies being used to ensure that the project did not permanently dislocate the communities' heritage resources and their beliefs. The use of EIA as a strategy to mediate between development projects and heritage protection proved effective in this and other projects where communities' well-being and identity were under threat.

What emerges from the brief review above is the need for a broader reading of the ways in which communities have constructed their knowledge systems over time and how they interact with their environments in creating systems of meaning. It is clear that the modern forms of knowledge and site protection systems imposed on local knowledge systems are sometimes inadequate in reflecting the heritage protection needs of communities and can bring discordance in the management of these heritage resources, thus undermining the long-term sustainability of any protection system.

The Botswana National Museum through its Natural History Division also confers protection on natural heritages such as plant species. From recent experiences in the undertaking of EIAs, it is quite clear that this task is daunting for the Museum despite its noble efforts. Recent experiences with the harvesting of plant resources and their exportation out of Botswana highlights some of the challenges faced by this authority in enforcing protection over heritage resources. What can be learned from the recent examples is the need to increase the coordination of material culture protection agencies and those which serve to protect non-material heritage such as traditional knowledge and natural resources. Clearly, the case of the exploitation of the traditional plant *Hoodia* demonstrated the challenges of commerce overtaking the interest of common use. One entity sought to make commercial gain from a natural heritage resource without due recourse to its sustainable use. Furthermore, the entry of a giant pharmaceutical company into the debate highlighted the challenges and the very fine line between harnessing communal knowledge and appropriation of such knowledge and natural resources for personal gain. It is likely that the Hoodia example will not be the first or the last. Other ongoing experiments in the area of food technology with the diverse production and processing of wild food plants such as Morula, Morama and Mosata, to mention a few, will continue to pose challenges for the protecting authorities and entrepreneurs who tap into communally held knowledge to develop commercially viable products (Kgarebe et al. 2003).

Heritage Protection and the Challenges of Tourism Development

Tourism as an industry developed only in the post-Second World War period and grew in the last three decades, particularly in its international dimensions. In southern Africa, the recognition of tourism as a potential contributor to national development took place very recently, as recently as the 1990s in countries like Botswana and South Africa. Several factors influenced this late development. The political situation in the region throughout the 1970s to the 1990s impacted negatively on international tourism. In Botswana, the need to diversify economic growth from the over-reliance on diamonds was articulated within the context of the National Development Plan 8 (1997/ 98–2002/3). As a result, the promotion of tourism in earnest is only gaining momentum within the region though there are still challenges to its growth. Botswana recently launched a national eco-tourism strategy to oversee the strategic development of eco-tourism (Botswana Government 2002).

The growth of tourism internationally has been directly linked to the consumption of heritage. People travel not only for environmental wilderness experiences but also to learn about other cultures and places. In Europe and America, many countries responded by marketing their heritage in ways which could attract tourists, as for example 'English Heritage'. America proved the most successful in its marketing of popular culture and modern amusement places. Africa attracts tourists principally for her wildlife and wilderness resources (for instance, the Victoria Falls and national parks in Kenya). Cultural resources, though often included in tourism, were not the main attraction, and local cultures and cultural products served as a backdrop to the marketing of 'the pristine African experience'. In southern Africa, cultural products marketed as curios (airport or commercial art), were the only interaction between international tourists and local communities.

The change in international conservation philosophies from the late 1960s saw the influence of environmental discourse on development agendas and the tourism industry. The influence of the Rio Convention and post-Rio discourses on environmental conservation also swayed public perceptions of environmental conservation. The notion of the 'green tourist' filtered into the promotion of tourism, with an increased realisation of the potential for marketing cultural heritage as part of the tourism experiences. Manyanga notes that 'the world-wide trend in the tourism industry today is the growing appetite for indigenous cultural experiences by the tourist' (Manyanga 2000: 160). That said, this relationship between tourism and cultural heritage is not a straightforward one. It is fraught with difficulties particularly in Southern Africa where development agendas and issues of heritage management and representation of local communities often come into direct conflict. The future of heritage tourism is yet to be clearly defined in terms of its benefits to communities and its sustainability.

In Southern Africa, development agendas have focussed on the reduction of poverty, particularly for rural populations, and the provision of stable governance institutions. In the search for avenues for increasing participation in development, some countries saw a niche in the emerging area of cultural heritage tourism as an avenue for enhancing community participation and diversification of production. This by and large included the production of crafts, the engagement of culture in its various media such as music, art and the marketing of archaeological and historic resources. In some countries such as Zimbabwe, the potential gains from this avenue were realised with the marketing of sites such as Great Zimbabwe, Victoria Falls and the Nyanga district. South Africa has aggressively marketed its heritage resources, which has ensured a steady growth of tourists to the country (Davison 1995).

Who Protects People Against Heritage Attrition?

Whilst efforts towards economic diversification in the region particularly in Botswana to embrace eco-tourism are commendable, it is clear that communities endure a number of losses along the way. Many communities which were hitherto protected either by their remoteness from highly urbanised areas are finding themselves thrust under the glare of the tourist's lens. Many tourists in search of the exotic or authentic seek out ever more remote or exotic communities which can be captured on film and noted in diaries in anticipation of a best-seller in the travel literature sections. Film and reality television productions of people travelling through lush jungles or bare deserts encountering a few 'natives' still capture the public imagination and force producers seeking ever better ratings for their productions to thrust in front of viewers ever more exotic 'discoveries' of relics of humankind.

It is clear that the continued consumption of the exotic is heavily biased towards the developing world as the object of consumption. This inevitably manifests itself in the production of new media such as films, literature and crafts reworked from their contexts to new owners eager to display their encounters with the vestiges of 'primitive humanity'. Ironically, the consumption of material culture and the intangible heritage of the developing world has also served to create solidarity movements in the developed world, where identification with the developing world has often been reflected in iconography such as the Ghanaian *kente* cloth in the African-American civil rights movement, Peruvian or other Latin American fabrics in Europe, or the renaissance of the 'German print' in urban South African fashion. These multiple appropriations of traditional cultural systems and their material products are therefore challenging to students of IKS who need to decipher a number of issues before drawing general conclusions on the basis of a few examples in the consumption of the heritage of southern Africa.

A number of countries in the region have attempted to bridge the gaps between tourism development and heritage protection. In South Africa, the recent revision of legislation and the resultant establishment of an Agency managing heritage have placed heritage management partly outside the ambit of direct state control (Abrahms 1989; SAHRA 2000). As Ndoro and Pwiti note, legislation developed in the region was in most cases biased towards the protection of European heritage or other resources selected by colonial officers. They state that:

> It appears that the pioneering protective legislation was not founded on an objective approach to preserve the diverse African cultural landscape but rather on protecting a few sites which served the interests of the early white settlers. The transfer of ownership of cultural property to government and the displacement of people in these areas meant that local communities no longer had legal access to the sites (Ndoro and Pwiti 2001: 32; Myles 1990: 122).

The legislation by and large attempted to identify and protect monuments and relics for public interest. The assumption was that the public would benefit from the long-term conservation of these sites and monuments. Whilst the underlying assumption is good in principle, the problem as noted above was that often the local communities had little participation in the process of identification of the monuments or their declaration as nationally significant places. This was also the case with the declaration of national parks and game reserves.

In Zimbabwe, the National Museums and Monuments of Zimbabwe are custodian of the Act governing the protection of archaeological sites and relics. The Act vests powers in the Director who can enforce penalties on those who violate the Act. This Act was promulgated in 1972 (Government of Zimbabwe) and carries with it heavy penalties for those who violate its provisions. Separate legislation governs the protection of wildlife and the environment. Other countries in the region such as Zambia (Katanweka 1995) also have legislation promulgated with more or less similar provisions as those cited above. The main intent of the legislation is to protect archaeological and other heritage.

One of the challenges of the legislation summarised above has been its definition of monuments in terms of time and place. As a result of constraints in resources, the legislation in most cases defines sites, relics or monuments, in terms of defined visible structures assigned a time period which also informs its scheduling status or significance. As a result, most legislation has focussed on early prehistoric or archaeological sites and recent historic or colonial monuments. In the main, the legislation remained silent on local heritage associated with indigenous or local communities. The legislation in most cases did not take into account local definitions of time, space or place, something which has resulted in conflicts in the management of sites. This observation is supported by Manyanga who notes that 'legislation currently in use in Zimbabwe on the protection of cultural heritage is prohibitive, hence silent on sacred sites and the continued use of a site by its traditional custodians' (Manyanga 1999: 11).

This omission in the legislation has resulted in an uneasy and sometimes conflict-ridden relationship between heritage managers and local communities who appropriate archaeological sites for their use as worship places and or sacred places. This continuous re-use of archaeological sites is a familiar sight to many heritage managers in Southern Africa. In Botswana, South Africa, Zimbabwe, and Zambia many rock art sites are re-used for healing, ritual rainmaking, initiation and other activities which are central to the world view of local communities. The intervention of archaeologists has sometimes resulted in conflict and vandalism of sites by locals (Pwiti 1996; Pwiti & Mvenge 1996). It is interesting to note that in Australia where similar problems existed, the Australian Archaeological Association took the positive step of including local Aboriginal communities in heritage planning to avoid the conflict which had come to make the practice of archaeology impossible in some states. Through the Burra Charter, Australia was able to provide for Aboriginal people to participate in long-term decision making about management of sites. Flood (1989: 83) notes that 'the need both to consult and to involve Aborigines in archaeology is very clear, and the ethical, philosophical, legal, social and political arguments in favour overwhelming'.

One of the challenges regarding the consultation of local communities in Southern Africa, particularly in Zimbabwe and possibly South Africa, has been the problem of contests relating to land. As noted by Zimbabwean archaeologists, the contests over land between local African communities and settler white communities have been a point of contention which has directly involved heritage managers. Flood further notes that:

> The land rights issues inevitably affect both cultural resources managers and archaeologists. Many landowners are reluctant to give permission for archaeo-logical research to be carried out on their property in case it leads to discovery of significant Aboriginal sites... Sites have even been deliberately destroyed by landowners in the course of this white backlash (Flood 1989: 83).

Similarly in Zimbabwe, the role of some sites as sacred or significant places during the period of resistance to colonialism, the liberation period and the post independence period has led to the politicisation of archaeological sites and heritage places like the Great Zimbabwe Ruins and Ntabazika Mambo, which are claimed by local communities as their traditional lands but are cur-rently in state protection or private land ownership (Manyanga 1999; 2000). In sum, the failure to thoroughly discuss the role and place of local commu-nities in the revision of Acts governing heritage means that there are still many contested issues between state heritage management agencies and local communities. For so long as local communities feel excluded in the process of managing their past(s), it will remain problematic to win their support in the promotion of tourism or tourism-related activities. This also places in jeopardy the safety of heritage resources which then become vulnerable to vandalism, as has been witnessed at many rock art sites in Botswana, South Africa and Zimbabwe.

The Gods' Resting Places

An area that still remains contentious is the area of marketing cultural prac-tices and places which in many cultures were, and still remain, sacred or of religious significance. Manyanga (1999: 190) argues that 'with some flexibility, the activities and involvement of the traditional groups can be put to good of both archaeology and tourism development'. This statement comes in the wake of experiences by Zimbabwe heritage management professionals de-bating the role of sites such as the Great Zimbabwe, Matopo Hills and Njelele sites which are also sites of ritual significance for a number of local commu-nities in Zimbabwe, Botswana and South Africa. He notes that pilgrimages from the three countries to Njelele shrine in itself creates a local tourism activity, though not so stated. However, given the negative impacts of these religious activities on the archaeological sites, heritage custodians have often been forced to intervene to safeguard them. This has sometimes created con-flict.

In Botswana, examples of sites where local beliefs and use of sites have conflicted with principles of heritage protection as provided in the Monuments and Relics Act include the sites of Matsieng in the Kgatleng district, the Tswapong hills, Lekhubu in the Boteti sub-district, and Tsodilo Hills in Ngamiland. Though the National Museum has attempted to ensure that the interests of communities are well represented in the management plans of these heritage sites, there are still problems in how communities access these places and the kinds of activities they can continue to carry out as part of their ritual practices.

As a solution, Manyanga proposes ways in which these activities can be marketed for a larger tourism market with a view to generating revenues for better protection and rehabilitation of sites. Whilst this provides a possible solution, it creates precedents which may have other implications as yet not well interrogated, particularly the intrusion into sacred or ritual activities. This may contribute to the commercialisation of practices which hold much higher significance as socio-religious practices within the world view of local communities than is currently understood. The assumption that the local communities will be ready for the impact of tourism at higher levels may need reviewing, particularly to ensure that there are adequate measures in place to ensure the integrity of such cultures and their practitioners.

Another case in point is the current debate over the Khoisan Cultural heritage. Whilst some people advocate retaining 'pristine' Khoisan cultural heritage institutions, others see this as a fallacy given the dynamic nature of all cultures. The idea of authenticity in any given cultural practice or presentation, particularly if it is geared towards tourism, becomes suspect. A related example is the recent development of a community tourism facility at Moremi Gorge in the Tswapong Hills. This community-run eco-tourism project promotes tourists' access to sacred pools in the Moremi Gorge whilst discouraging local young people from visiting the area. Camping facilities are under construction at the base of the Hill and it remains to be seen how this will affect the sanctity of the area once people camp overnight at the site.

International heritage protection legislation

Over and above national legislation protecting heritage, Southern African countries have the support of various pieces of international legislation, particularly the illicit trade in cultural properties. UNESCO has led the way, with UN agencies promulgating Conventions for the protection of cultural heritage. One key Convention is the 1970 Convention on the Means of Prohibiting and Preventing the Illicit Import, Export, and Transfer of Ownership of Cultural Property. The UNESCO Convention concerning the Protection of the World Cultural and Natural Heritage (1972) elaborates international provisions for the provision of cultural heritage. Southern African countries which are signatories to this and other Conventions enjoy the protection of their national heritage at an international level. The UNESCO World Heritage Sites Programme also allowed for the selection of heritage sites of magnificent or 'wonders of the world' status to be protected for global posterity. This selection of sites has proved contentious with many feeling that it is inherently biased towards European architectural structures.

Other international efforts under the UN include the role of ICOM (International Council of Museums), whose Charter of 1990 for the Protection and Management of Archaeological Heritage reinforced national legislation aimed at protecting cultural heritage. Likewise, ICOMOS (International Council on Monuments and Sites) through its Committee ICAHM (International Committee on Archaeological Heritage Management) was able to assist international efforts in the training of human resources, the provision of resources for creating public awareness, and other forms of support for the conservation and protection of monuments. ICCROM (International Centre for the Study of the Preservation and Restoration of Cultural Property) and more recently AFRICOM have enhanced training and capacity building for heritage managers, particularly in the southern African region. These international efforts have focussed on building expertise in the conservation and management of cultural property and as mentioned above, have not directly dealt with the broader concerns of intangible heritage (which is expressed in many traditional societies) as part of the tangible heritage. This aspect is, however, more recently being addressed by UNESCO through its Conventions on Intangible Heritage.

Reconciling the Legal and the Local: Building Bridges in Heritage Protection in Botswana and the Region

Several key points emerge from the foregoing overview:

- There are still areas within legislation both in Botswana and regionally which need re-definition or revision to include the views and interests of local communities;

- There is a need for increasing coordination within public service departments charged with the protection of heritage in their management of heritage resources, including people. This should also be extended to the partnerships created with the private sector and civil society organisations in developing strategies for protecting heritage resources to avoid conflicting interests, use and appropriation of knowledge in the course of development projects;

- Concerns about capacity to implement within custodian departments and agencies are real and need to be addressed in terms of funding and human resource development to effectively implement legislation. Although resources exist internationally such as those provided by UNESCO and WIPO, the rapid changes in the production and use of information often results with developing country communities losing out to those who can exploit, patent first or faster. To this end, the resolutions of the World Summit for Sustainable Development which in the main sought to ensure equitable partnerships between development donors and beneficiaries must be followed up and the implementations of such resolutions pursued through forums such as NEPAD and the African Union (AU) for the African continent.

- The niche for cultural heritage development within tourism development exists in the region but it needs to be well articulated in tourism policies and to take on board concerns about the dangers of commercialisation of local cultures. For heritage tourism to be sustainable, it has to demonstrate its grounding within community development platforms as has been innovated in models such as the CBNRMP or CAMPFIRE projects in Botswana and Zimbabwe respectively. Though these projects have had their limitations, they were important in showing how development projects can take on board community knowledge systems and have the capacity to embrace community innovation and creativity whilst building capacity.

In the last decade, South Africa in particular has articulated and marketed cultural tourism in its promotion of the 'Rainbow Nation' concept. Though contentious, many have felt the positive impact of this venture insofar as making South Africa's cultural diversity globally visible. The branding of the product 'Proudly South African' has evoked a consciousness within many South African and indeed Batswana to interrogate their identity and the ways in which this identity has been developed, marketed and exported beyond the borders of South Africa. Eco-tourism as the marketing and direct sale of cultural products such as curios, airport art or other outstanding works of art, has been reviewed elsewhere in terms of its potential benefit to local communities. What might be emphasised here is the positive step towards protecting the rights of cultural entrepreneurs in the music and other industries through the promulgation of laws such as the Botswana Copyright and Neighbouring Rights Act 2000. These Acts enhance the protection of intangible heritage by protecting individual artists or cultural producers.

A Cultural Heritage Resources Management Programme Model

Botswana, through the Department of Wildlife and National Parks, proposed and implemented a project called Community Based Natural Resources Management Programme (CBNRMP) (Cassidy & Madzwamuse 1999a; 1999b) which principally aimed at attaining community participation in the management of wildlife resources. The programme has been reviewed elsewhere and suffice to say that in its national implementation it provided a model for the management of cultural and heritage resources in Botswana and, by extension, in the region. Zimbabwe already had a successful experience with the Communal Areas Management Programme for Indigenous Resources (CAMPFIRE). These models have demonstrated that effective community participation in issues of development and resource management are possible. They have also, with the aid of partner donor organisations, ensured training and capacity building at local levels within communities.

There has been a growing academic debate over the role of indigenous knowledge systems in contributing to development in the twenty-first century (Odora-Hoppers 2002). It is argued here that IKS, as articulated in academic programmes or development agendas, illustrates the feasibility of rich CBNRM programmes. Since many communities are already imparting knowledge to scientific communities, tourists and other audiences, the development of cultural resources management programmes can go hand in hand with other development projects for the direct benefit of communities.

Conclusion

This paper has reviewed the development of heritage protection legislation and practices at the global and local levels in the context of southern Africa. What has been observed is the strong influence of Euro-American traditions in the current practice of heritage management in the region. Further, the legacies of colonialism and the unequal access to resources in the post-colonial era have continued to marginalise communities' participation in heritage management. One of the key issues fuelling problems in managing heritage resources, particularly archaeological heritage, has been the re-use of sites and monuments for traditional ceremonies by local communities. The role of archaeologists and other heritage managers as protectors, mediators, interpreters and presenters of heritage has emerged as an important one, particularly their role in ensuring the representation of local views and access to heritage resources. One of the key challenges to local communities participating in tourism even in its people-friendly form is the manner in which their participation will ensure their protection first as people with basic human and cultural rights, and secondly as entrepreneurs. It is argued that without prior training, skills and understanding of global dynamics and markets of cultural enterprise, many communities may stand to lose more that they gain.

References

Abrahams, G., 1989, 'A Review of the South African Cultural Heritage Legislation 1987', in Cleere H., ed., *Archaeological Heritage Management in the Modern World*, London, Unwin Hyman, pp. 205-218.

Andah, B., ed., 1990, *Cultural Resources Management: An African Dimension*, Ibadan, Wisdom Press.

Ascherson, N., 2000, 'Editorial', *Public Archaeology*, 1 (1), pp.1-4.

Botswana Government, 2001, Monuments and Relics Act, Gaborone, Government Printer.

Botswana Government, 2001, National Policy on Culture, Gaborone, Government Printer.

Botswana Government, 2002. Botswana National Eco-tourism Strategy, Gaborone, Government Printer.

Campbell, A., 1998, 'Archaeology in Botswana: Its origins and growth', in P.J. Lane et al., eds., *Ditswa Mmung: The Archaeology of Botswana*, Gaborone, Pula Press, 24-49.

Cassidy, L., and Madzwamuse, M., 1999a, eds., *Community Mobilisation in Community-Based Natural Resources Management in Botswana*, Gaborone, IUCN.

Cassidy, L., and Madzwamuse, M., 1999b, eds., *Enterprise Development and Community Based Natural Resource Management in Botswana*.

Cleere, H., 1989, 'Introduction: The Rationale of Archaeological Heritage Management', in Cleere, H., ed., *Archaeological Heritage Management*, London, Unwin Hyman, pp.1-19.

Davison, P., 1995, ' The Heritage of African settlement in South Africa', in D. Munjeri et al., eds., *African Cultural Heritage and the World Heritage Convention*, UNESCO, pp.90-95.

Denbow, J. 2002; 2003, personal communications.

Flood, J., 1989, '"Tread Softly for you Tread on my Bones": The Development of Cultural Resources Management in Australia', in Cleere, H., ed., *Archaeological Heritage Management*, pp.79-101.

Katanweka, N., 1995, 'Illicit Traffic of Cultural Property in Zambia: A Profile', in ICOM, ed., *Illicit Traffic of Cultural Property in Africa*, pp.189-197.

Kgarebe, B., A. Segobye, and R. Cordner, 2003, 'Indigenous Knowledge and Intellectual Property: Challenges for the Developing Country Societies', Unpublished paper presented at the World Intellectual Property Day Celebrations, Gaborone.

Kiyaga-Mulindwa, D., and Segobye, A., 1995, 'Archaeology and Education in Botswana', in Stone P., and B. Molyneaux, eds., *The Presented past: Heritage, Museums and Education*, London, Routledge, pp. 46-60.

Lowenthal, D., 1985, *The Past Is a Foreign Country*, Cambridge, Cambridge University Press.

Lowenthal, D.,1990, 'Conclusion: Archaeologists and Others', in Gathercole P., & D. Lowenthal, eds., *The Politics of the Past*, London, Unwin Hyman, pp.302-314.

Manyanga, M., 1999, 'The Antagonism of Living Realities: Archaeology and Religion the Case of Manyanga (NtabazikaMambo) National Monument', *Zimbabwea*, (6) pp.10-14.

Manyanga, M. 2000, 'Tourism and Cultural Heritage: Controversy on key tourist destinations in Zimbabwe', in Robinson, M., et al., *Expressions of Culture, Identity and Meaning in Tourism*, pp.183-193.

Munjeri, D., 1995, 'Spirit of the People, Nerve of Heritage', in Munjeri, D., et al., eds., *African Cultural Heritage and the World Heritage Convention*, UNESCO, pp.52-58.

Myles, K., 1989, 'Cultural Resources Management in Sub-Saharan Africa: Nigeria, Togo and Ghana', in Cleere, H., ed., *Archaeological Heritage Management*, pp.118-127.

Ndoro, W., and G. Pwiti, 2001, 'Heritage management in southern Africa: local, national and international discourses', *Public Archaeology*, 2(1), pp.21-34.

Ndoro, W., 2001, *Your Monument our Shrine: The Preservation of Great Zimbabwe*, Uppsala, Studies in African Archaeology, 19.

Odora , Hoppers C., 2002, 'Indigenous Knowledge and the Integration of Knowledge Systems', in C. Odora Hoppers, ed., *Indigenous Knowledge and the Integration of indigenous Knowledge Systems*, Claremont, New Africa Books, pp. 2-22.

Parsons, N., and Segobye, A., 2001, 'Missing persons and stolen bodies: the repatriation of El Negro to Botswana', in C. Fforde et. al., eds., *The Dead and Their Possessions: Repatriation inPrinciple, Policy and Practice*, London, Routledge, pp. 245-255.

Pressouyre, L., 1995, 'Cultural heritage and the 1972 Convention: Definition and Evolution of a Concept', in D. Munjeri et al., eds., *African Cultural Heritage and the World Heritage Convention*, UNESCO, pp.13-19.

Pwiti, G. and Mvenge, G., 1996, 'Archaeologists,Tourists and Rainmakers: Problems in the Management of Rock Art Sites in Zimbabwe, a Case Study of Domboshava National Monument', in Pwiti, G. and Soper, R., eds., *Aspects of African Archaeology*, Harare, University of Zimbabwe Publications, pp.817-823.

Pwiti, G. and Soper, R., eds., 1996, *Aspects of African Archaeology*, Harare, University of Zimbabwe Publications.

Schmidt, P., and McIntosh, R. J., eds., 1996, *Plundering Africa's Past*, London, James Currey.

Segobye, A., 2001, 'Missing Persons: Stolen Bodies and Patrimony Issues in Botswana, the El Negro Story', *Pula* vol. 16 (1), pp.14-18.

UNESCO, 1998, *World Heritage Document*, Paris, UNESCO Publications.

7

The Development of Indigenous Knowledge Systems Policy and Legislation in South Africa: Intellectual Property Implications for Knowledge Holders and Practitioners

Mogege Mosimege

Initial Developments in Indigenous Knowledge Systems in South Africa

The Indigenous Knowledge Systems (IKS) Programme and related activities as presently understood and conceptualised in South Africa can be traced to an idea which was discussed by the Chairperson of the Parliamentary Portfolio Committee of Arts, Culture, Science and Technology and some members of the top management at the Council for Scientific and Industrial Research (CSIR) towards the end of 1996. This discussion resulted in a decision to carry out a survey in the Provinces of Limpopo and Mpumalanga in South Africa. A pilot to conduct a survey of indigenous technologies in these two provinces was commissioned from the University of The North by the CSIR. After a workshop was organised at the University to report back on the findings of the audit, decisions were made by stakeholders present at the workshop to roll out similar audits to other provinces in South Africa. The roll out involved an average of forty students and four members of staff at each of the nine universities that participated. These audits were carried out by universities which are classified as Historically Disadvantaged Universities (HDU), at times referred to as Historically Black Universities (HBU). This process is generally referred to as the national audit of indigenous technologies in South Africa. Each participating institution also conducted a workshop in the period between 1997 and 1998 to report back on its findings. These provincial workshops culminated in the first National Workshop on IKS in September 1998 at the University of North West.

The objectives of the IKS audits were as follows:

(i) Identify different indigenous technologies in the different communities in South Africa and compile a record;

(ii) Compile a national database of the technologies which could be updated at different stages when other related projects are engaged in;

(iii) Explore and investigate these technologies to determine those that have potential to be developed into business enterprises for possible job creation;

(iv) Assist the indigenous technologists and other community members in the development of the technologies into business enterprises;

(v) Establish a policy on the research and interaction with the different communities for the advancement of work on Indigenous Knowledge Systems;

(vi) Establish legislation for the protection of Intellectual Property which will protect both the researchers and the community within which the research is done;

(vii) Capacity building for the students and the research team members in interacting with indigenous technologists and the communities from which the technologists come;

(viii) Provision of assistance for members of the communities in business development skills in relation to the different technologies;

(ix) Training of members of staff and in some cases students in Microsoft Access Database; and

(x) Training of students in research methods for interaction with communities.

Reflecting on the objectives of the audit, it may be concluded that some of them were easier to attain, whereas others have proved very difficult. Those objectives that can be regarded as fairly well attained are (i), (ii), (ix), and (x). Those that can be regarded as minimally or partly attained are (iii), (v), (vi), (vii) and (viii). Very little was achieved in terms of objective (iv).

It was probably very ambitious to hope that all the above objectives and those that were partly attained could be achieved by an audit which at most was very superficial in terms of revealing all the necessary details regarding the different indigenous technologies. However, what can be regarded as the greatest achievement of the audit, which was not even thought about as a possibility at its conceptualisation, is the extent to which conscientisation about

IKS has been raised and debates on IKS have been started. Since the audit, debates in IKS have increased and permeated most of the South African society. The following activities relating to IKS have taken place at regular intervals since the audit: meetings, seminars, workshops, forums, brainstorming sessions, researches and debates on funding and co-ordination.

These developments have also made it necessary for the Department of Science and Technology to embark on the process of developing policy and legislation for the recognition, promotion, development, protection, and affirmation of the indigenous knowledge. The development of both the policy and legislation took into account the debates and the experiences that came out of the audits and used these to inform further development of both processes.

Research on the Intellectual Property Needs and Expectations of Knowledge Holders by the World International Property Organization (WIPO)

At the same time as the developments in IKS in South Africa were starting to take shape, steps were being taken at an international level with respect to IKS. Between June 1998 and November 1999, the World Intellectual Property Organisation (WIPO), conducted a total of nine fact-finding missions (FFMs) to twenty-eight countries in the South Pacific, Southern Africa, Eastern Africa, West Africa, South Asia, North America, Central America, South America, Arab Countries, and the Caribbean (WIPO, 2001). These fact-finding missions were designed to enable WIPO to identify, as far as possible, the IP needs and expectations of traditional knowledge holders. The FFM to Southern Africa took place from 4-20 September 1998 in the following countries: Uganda, Tanzania, Namibia and South Africa. In South Africa, it coincided with the First National Workshop on IKS which took place at the University of North West from 3-5 September 1998.

Views expressed with respect to the use of IP to protect traditional knowledge may be categorised as follows:

- *IP will be ineffective in protecting TK*: Many expressed doubts that the IP systems in their countries could serve as an effective tool for the protection of new subject matter such as TK. The need for TK holders to be able to enforce any measures to protect TK was stressed many times.

- *IP is unsuitable as a means to protect TK*: Some people were also critical of the present IP system. They believed that the system is unsuitable as a modality to protect TK because of what they regarded as the system's private property, exclusive rights and individual author or inventor-centric nature.

- *IP can be used to protect TK*: Most TK holders consulted had little or no information on the IP system. Many requests were made for more information and for training on the IP system, particularly on options it may offer for the protection of TK for the benefit of TK holders. It is recognised that some forms of TK are already protected by the IP system.

These FFMs also resulted in the establishment of the Intergovernmental Committee on Intellectual Property and Genetic Resources, Traditional Knowledge and Folklore (IGC), which convened meetings of member states after April 2001. The IGC was established by the WIPO General Assembly in October 2000 as an international forum for debate and dialogue concerning the interplay between intellectual property (IP) and traditional knowledge, genetic resources, and folklore (cultural expressions). The Committee's work programme has considered both the defensive and the positive protection of traditional knowledge. For example:

(i) A study on the operational definitions relevant to TK;

(ii) A review of existing national systems of intellectual property for TK;

(iii) An analysis of the elements for a possible *sui generis* system for the protection of TK;

(iv) The use of database to promote defensive protection;

(v) The development of an IP Management Toolkit for the documentation of TK.

The fifth meeting of the IGC took place in July 2003 at which these was deadlock with respect to an internationally binding instrument on traditional knowledge. The debates at these meetings have always pitted the developed against the developing countries, and so it is understandable that a deadlock would ultimately be reached as the finalisation of such an instrument challenged the practices and exploitation of IKS by the developed countries without necessarily benefiting the knowledge holders in the developing countries. An internationally binding instrument with respect to IKS would start the process of challenging such practices and curb the wanton destruction of the indigenous knowledge and related natural resources. The lack of international consensus on the substance of an internationally acceptable regime of protection is to be expected as 'the countries endowed with genetic resources, traditional knowledge and folklore seek to secure protection for such resources, while the user countries are bound to be reluctant to submit to additional restraints on innovating and creating in ways that conform to existing intellectual property agreements' (Weeraworawit 2003).

Developments with Respect to Policy and Legislation on IKS

The Draft IKS Policy

A Policy on IKS in South Africa has been in the process of development since 2000. Its development built on the earlier work of the Parliamentary Portfolio Committee on Arts, Culture, Science and Technology; the Audit of indigenous technologies; the work of the Science Councils IKS Champions; the delegations of the Department of Arts, Culture, Science and Technology to India and China on fact-finding missions and best practice learning; the drafts of Policy and Legislation by the Task Team and the Review Teams, both comprising of representatives from Science Councils, Government Departments, Legal Practitioners, and IKS Holders. Some of these developments have been reported in the 'Prolegomena to a Policy on Indigenous Knowledge Systems' (Deliwe 1998). The prolegomena also records the classification of IKS in the context of South Africa and elaborates on such classifications and their implications for the definitions and further development of IKS.

The draft policy is an enabling framework ensuring that indigenous people are able to realise their full potential in society, and constitutes a basis for the successful achievement of all other national goals and aspirations. This policy has been developed in the context of the National System of Education and Innovation. The integration of IKS with Western and other systems of innovation and its integration in the National Qualifications Framework provide the platform for formulating a coherent policy position of IKS in the National System of Innovation. The policy framework also proceeds from the premise that innovation is an all-embracing notion based on the production and creative application of knowledge which will demand a national research policy integrated with the National Research and Development Strategy and cross-sectoral cooperation with its strategic stakeholders.

The Policy is based on the four key drivers in the context of South Africa:

(i) Affirmation of African cultural values in the face of globalisation;

(ii) Development of services provided by indigenous knowledge holders and practitioners involved in traditional medicine, technologies, spirituality and cosmo-vision, indigenous languages, and other related areas on indigenous knowledge;

(iii) Contribution of indigenous knowledge to the economy - the role of indigenous knowledge in employment and wealth creation is regarded as very important;

(iv) Interfacing of IKS with other knowledge systems. Increasingly, indigenous knowledge is used together with modern biotechnology in the pharmaceutical and other sectors, dependent on innovation.

Some of the highlights of the draft policy are:

(i) The principles of good governance and administrative practice, which inform all initiatives on IKS and related activities;

(ii) The identification and establishment of institutional mechanisms (National Advisory Council; the National IKS Office; the National Development Trust Fund);

(iii) The principles of funding and financing of IKS activities (Research, Projects, Capacity Building for IKS Holders, etc,); and

(iv) A coherence and consistency in Government's approach in aligning the IKS Policy with other regulatory policies and authorities within government, getting the Policy Framework on the agenda of other policies.

The IKS Policy has reached final stages of development and will be presented to Parliament after the national elections next year.

The Draft IKS Bill

The challenges facing the development of any Bill for the protection of IKS are enormous. The South African IKS Bill aims to recognise, promote, develop, protect and affirm the hitherto undermined and marginalised IKS, to contribute to the reclamation and realisation on indigenous knowledge of South Africa's diverse communities and value systems connected therewith; and to establish a regulatory framework for IKS and matters connected therewith.

The Objectives of the Bill are:

(i) To give legal recognition to IK and IKS and IK practitioners;

(ii) To establish principles to guide and manage the recognition, promotion, development, innovation and protection of IK and IKS;

(iii) To regulate forms of ownership and benefit sharing of IK and IKS at all levels of value addition;

(iv) To provide for sound governance in the protection and development of IK and IKS;

(v) To provide for the development of code of ethics, conduct and good practice for owners, producers, managers and users of IK and IKS;

(vi) To facilitate ways for making claims for reparation and compensation for IK and IKS that have hitherto been appropriated on the basis of the principles of unjust enrichment;

(vii) To provide mechanisms for the capacity building of IK practitioners including education, training and development;

(viii) To promote research and development activities in the area of IK and IKS;

(ix) To promote public awareness of IK and IKS; and

(x) To establish a regulatory mechanism called the Indigenous Knowledge Systems Authority to assist in achieving the above.

The IKS Bill has taken much longer to develop, even longer than the Policy. This has been due to the complexity of debates related to the protection of IKS and the related intellectual property, and other developments related to IKS. The lead Department on IKS (Department of Science and Technology) has also concentrated and moved further on the Policy as opposed to the Bill. It is hoped that the Bill will once more gain momentum after the Policy has been accepted by the South African Cabinet. It will certainly have to take into account the following developments which have taken place or are taking place in other departments and will possibly have been concluded at the time of the resumption of further work on the Bill.

A Biodiversity Bill has been developed by the Department of Environmental Affairs and Tourism. The Department of Health has drawn up a Traditional Health Practitioners Bill. The Traditional Leadership and Governance Framework Bill has been developed by the Department of Provincial and Local Government. Amendments to the Copyright and Patent Laws are presently being reviewed by the Department of Trade and Industry.

Another development that has taken place in South Africa has been the establishment of the Intergovernmental Committee on IKS in 2002. This is a Committee that comprises the following departments: Science and Technology; Education; Trade and Industry; Health; Environmental Affairs and Tourism; Land Affairs; Agriculture; Water Affairs; Provincial and Local Government; and Foreign Affairs. Other departments that have been invited or are still to be invited are Arts and Culture, and Sports and Recreation. This development recognises that no one department can adequately deal with the issues surrounding IKS, even at a policy and legislation development level. This committee has contributed immensely to the development of various pieces of legislation mentioned earlier. Without proper coordination between these departments, the chances of working at cross purposes can be very high.

Conclusion: Intellectual Property Implications for Knowledge Holders

Whenever issues related to IKS are discussed, they bring to the fore intellectual property questions. A lot of research has been done by researchers from a variety of institutions – tertiary institutions like universities and technikons, science councils, pharmaceutical and other companies – on various forms of indigenous knowledge. In South Africa, the research, especially by tertiary institutions, has increased after a ring-fenced amount of money was set aside by the Department of Science and Technology since 2000 and made available to researchers through the National Research Foundation. These forms of research give rise to questions of who actually owns the knowledge. Is it the researchers or is it the indigenous technologists? A related question that goes along with this one is who actually benefits from all this research? Are the scales not tipped to a greater extent in favour of the researchers and scientists who, for the most of the time, are the major beneficiaries of this research? When the research has been done and the various forms of indigenous knowledge are recorded and published, does anything accrue to the communities about whom the research was conducted?

It is well known that indigenous knowledge is largely unprotected. This then results, as has happened over many years, in the exploitation of this knowledge by various multinational companies, without any benefits accruing to the custodians of the knowledge. 'African countries should look critically into the modalities of patenting their leading national biological diversity products and knowledge in order to protect the indigenous scientists, farmers, communities and herbalists from exploitation by people from outside the region' (Sofowora 1999: 22). This author is referring to the questions I have raised earlier about who benefits and who should actually be patenting whatever results from the vast knowledge of the indigenous technologists and knowledge holders in general.

The Convention on Biological Diversity, 1992, appropriately put the knowledge of indigenous people at centre-stage. As the Intellectual Property Policy Directorate noted (1998: 2), the Convention 'recognised the role of indigenous peoples, their knowledge and their practices in the conservation and sustainable use of genetic resources'. The Convention called for the recognition of communal ownership of Intellectual Property (Deliwe, 1998: 14). This recognition has raised significant questions concerning the protection of indigenous knowledge and practices through some form of intellectual property rights system, as well as the goal of ensuring appropriate rewards for the use of such knowledge by others in developing products and processes.

The draft legislation which started in 1998, aimed at the Protection and Promotion of Intellectual Property in IKS, has still not been concluded. The length of time that it has taken during the process significantly shows that issues relating to the Intellectual Property in IKS are far from simple. In fact, during the public hearings on the draft legislation which were conducted in 2000, some of the comments showed support for the extension of intellectual property rights to indigenous knowledge. Those who supported this position argued that 'protecting indigenous knowledge through intellectual property rights would promote technological innovation and would facilitate the development and dissemination of that knowledge in the modern economic space', and those who advocated the retention of the status quo where such knowledge is treated as public good argued that 'the extension of intellectual property rights to indigenous knowledge would destroy the social basis for generating and managing the knowledge' (Portfolio Committee of Arts, Culture, Science and Technology, 2000: 5). The contrasting views of South Africans in this matter show that Intellectual Property concerns in relation to IKS are not necessarily an easy matter to resolve, and therefore it will take a much more concerted effort to put legislation in place which can, for the first time, adequately protect the knowledge and rights of the custodians of indigenous knowledge in South Africa.

References

Deliwe, M., 1998, 'Prolegomena to a Policy Framework on Indigenous Knowledge Systems in South Africa', Pretoria, CSIR.

Intellectual Property Policy Directorate, 1998, *The Biodiversity Convention, Intellectual property Rights, and Ownership of Genetic Resources: International Developments*, Canada.

Mosimege, M. D., 2001, 'The Developments and Challenges Facing the Indigenous Knowledge Systems Programme: South African Experiences', Paper Presented at an International Conference on Indigenous Knowledge Systems, Saskatoon, Canada, the University of Saskatchewan.

Portfolio Committee on Arts, Culture, Science and Technology, 2000, *Report on Public Hearings in Indigenous Knowledge Systems*, Cape Town.

Sofowora, A., 1999, 'Medicinal Plants Research in Africa: Prospects and Problems', in L. Makhubu, R. Mshana, O. Amusan, K. Adenji, D. Otieno and J. Msonthi, eds., *Procedings of the Symposium on African Medicinal and Indigenous Food Plants & The Role of Traditional Medicine in Health Care*, University of Swaziland.

Weeraworawit, W., 2003, 'International Legal Protection for Genetic Resources, Traditional Knowledge and Folklore: Challenges for the Intellectual Property System', in C. Bellmann, G. Dutfield and R. Melendez-Ortiz, eds., *Trading in Knowledge: Development Perspectives on TRIPS, Trade and Sustainability*, London, Earthscan Publications Ltd.

WIPO, 2001, *Intellectual Property Needs and Expectations of Traditional Knowledge Holders: WIPO Report on Fact-Finding Missions on Intellectual Property and Traditional Knowledge (1998–1999)*, Geneva.

8

Intellectual Property Rights and Natural Resources: A Case Study of Harvesters of Medicinal Plants in the North-West Province, South Africa

Otsile Ntsoane

Introduction

Protecting the interest of the poor people in developing countries has become part of the agenda of the World Bank and many donors from the West Reports from the World Bank indicate that there is potential in the exploitation of the bio-diversity of developing countries. This bio-diversity constitutes the riches and wealth of knowledge accumulated over thousands years through trials. Developing countries are in a position to invest in their own economies, in their own cultural heritage. However, a cognitively imperial education and skewed developmental theories have made it almost impossible for this to happen. The history of mental slavery and colonial mentality has made African countries take longer than expected after independence and freedom to realise the economic potential and social relevance of indigenous knowledge and its related technologies. The poverty that is currently experienced amidst the millionaires and well-off Africans is a sign of imbalances and of the inequality that exists. The causes of their existence are built upon the capitalist notion of individualism. Although we Africans find it hard to deal with the growing inequality, we understand the historical factors that put us into the bucket of imperialism and neo-colonialism.

Local Farmers and Gatherers

Little attention has been given to the potential impact of market methods (intellectual property or contracts) on local farming communities or indigenous peoples (Brush and Stabinsky 1996). Bio-piracy, collective rights, and intellectual property rights have a bearing on the scale of poverty currently experienced in Africa. The poverty-creating impact of bio-piracy and bio-prospecting can only be perceived if one recognises that there is a difference between the material economy and the financial economy. If people have rich bio-diversity and intellectual wealth, they can meet their needs for health care and nutrition through their own resources and their knowledge (Shiva 1997). If on the other hand, the rights to both resources and knowledge have been transferred from the community to IPR holders, the members of a community end up paying a high price or royalty for what was originally theirs and which they had for free. There is an argument that IPR make people materially poorer.

The nature of the intellectual property rights regime has not yet been understood by many people in developing countries. Scholars in many developing countries have differed with their governments on the issue of intellectual property rights regimes. They have expressed a number of concerns (Vandana Shiva 1997, 2000 and 1987).

The main concern is the involvement of corporations which commercialise the bio-diversity and transforms it into a proprietary knowledge patentable and protected by Western-style Intellectual Property Rights (IPR) regime. For example, here are some of the outcomes of this situation:

- Monopoly control over the bio-diversity and knowledge can be experienced once there is a law prohibiting free receiving and exchange between the individuals and the communities;

- Any bio-diversity that is commercialised is subject to exploitation. The focus shifts from feeding the local to satisfying the quest of the greedy outsider. The result is scarcity and sky-rocketing prices;

- Extinction can easily be seen due to over-exploitation;

- The local community will lose access and its rightful share to the plant once it is protected by IPR; and

- The local communities end up depending on commercial interests.

There are those who support the need for introducing Intellectual Property Rights on the basis of ethical and utilitarian rationales. According to Goldman (1989), the ethical argument refers to the notion that there exists a natural or moral right for a person to profit from ideas generated. The utilitarian argument refers to the notion that society benefits from allowing another person to monopolise one's own ideas. Going back to the ethical argument, its proponents posit that indigenous people have property rights to ideas as products of their labour, and since intellectual property exists in industrial and Western societies, it is only fair that it be available to people in other societies. The challenge is that the seed and pharmaceutical companies do not treat knowledge of biological diversity in the same way as local people. The former sees property and the later sees common good. The ethical argument was debunked and it is claimed that its failure lies on the findings that (i) it undermined the notion that ideas are property by some natural or moral right. The question that can be posed is why protect practical and not theoretical ideas. (ii) If property is a natural right then no one should be denied access to it.

The problem raised in the ethical and moral argument states that intellectual property rights are finite. This leaves us with the utilitarian argument and its justification that IP will increase inventiveness and innovation. The two are also challenged by other researchers. Shiva (2001) states that: 'the patent regimes that are designed and shaped could reintroduce a new era of colonialism in which not only are we recolonized as a people, but all life forms are colonized.' He further states that: 'we could challenge the patent paradigm that allows life forms to be treated as human inventions and corporate property, which allows piracy of centuries of innovation and indigenous creativity'.

What Is Africa's Take on IPR?

An international Conference on Trade Related Aspects of Intellectual Property Rights (TRIPS) on and the Convention on Biological Diversity (CBD) organised by the African Centre for Technology Studies was held in Nairobi in 1999. At this Conference, several observations were made that affect Africa. Africa needs technical assistance for the implementation of the TRIPS agreement. It was also noted that African countries have now an opportunity to develop common negotiating positions and strategies for the review of TRIPS, present and future reviews of WTO agreements, and that particular attention should be given to this (Dutfield, 2000). It was further observed that as Contracting Parties to the CBD they have established a set of obligations and principles to assert their sovereign rights over genetic resources, and to protect and promote the rights of their traditional and local communities. They now face the challenge of ensuring that the WTO regime gives more than symbolic regard to the principle of sustainable development and provisions of the CBD and related international instruments such as the International Undertaking on Plant Genetic Resources and the Convention for the Protection of New Varieties of Plants, 1961 (UPOV).

The following steps are suggested:

- Informed consultation at the national level should be organised by various groups, bringing together government, trade, agriculture, intellectual property, and CDB negotiators;

- The existing African regional bodies such as the African Union, NEPAD, African Regional Industrial Property Organisation (ARIPO) should mobilise international scholars and a variety of other entities to develop common African negotiating positions and strategies for the review; and

- Efforts should be made to build an indigenous capability to gather and analyse data on a wide range of public policy issues emerging from the inter-linked complexities of global regulatory regimes. In the view of the present author, this workshop is working towards these steps which should result in complete national policy and legislation by SADC on IPR in the near future.

Sharing with others: The Mataatua Declaration

The Mataatua Declaration, concerning Cultural and Intellectual Property Rights of Indigenous Peoples, was signed in New Zealand in 1993 and its preamble reads: 'Adopt or strengthen appropriate policies and or legal instruments that will protect indigenous intellectual and cultural property and the right to preserve customary and administrative systems and practices'. The Declaration recommended a number of positive steps to be considered in the development of policies and practices by indigenous peoples (Lalibertte, Settee, Waldran et al., 2001).

Indigenous People are expected to:

(i) Note that existing protection mechanisms are insufficient for the protection of Indigenous People's intellectual and cultural property rights;

(ii) Develop a code of ethics which external users must observe when recording (visual, audio, written) their traditional and customary knowledge; and

(iii) Assess existing legislation with respect to the protection of antiquities.

Narratives from the Field: Cassel

Ms Hilda Motshoari, a retired teacher, is knowledgeable about human rights and women's issues. She has organised a number of women and men into a village project harvesting Devils' Claw (*Sengaparile*). During the off season the women engage themselves with sewing projects. Ms Motshoari, a winner of MmaAfrika Awards for community service, speaks with confidence about how she defends the rights of the labourers involved in the project. She said they should be treated with human sensitivity. They should not be overlooked because they too contribute to the pride of the province.

Her narrative in the field included how she will make whites feel uncomfortable when they try to take the plant without paying a reasonable price. In some instances, whites would arrive and say that government wants to purchase the 'mother tuber' of the devil's claw. 'This is nonsense since they want to pay R150 per kg', she said. She regards the medicinal plant as the gold and diamonds of Cassel. She thought that the buyers should increase the price to R500, but after consultation and weeks thereafter the buyers with the middlemen returned to the village to buy the Devils Claw's mother tuber for R400. That was R100 less. She is not in favour of selling the tuber, saying it takes away the power of the community. The tuber is the source of the plant. When you remove it you leave the communities that depend on the plant powerless. She then describes how the middleman enters the village. The middleman would first go to Department of Agriculture and Conservation, Vryburg Office, as an entry point and ask for the *Sengaparile* project. A staff member would accompany the middleman to Cassel. On arrival the middlemen put up his own price for *Sengaparile*. At times a wet tuber or whole tuber would be sold for R600 per kg. But she insists that without her strong understanding of both the English and Afrikaans languages and training in the harvesting, management and development of the plant, the people might have ended up robbed by the middleman. Her understanding of these languages helps a great deal when negotiating.

The buyers tried to convince her to sell at lower price. The mark up from R8-60 or R7-60 to R21 for Devils Claw per kg shows that the previous buyer was cheating the community. The one who came to buy put up his price at R8-50, then came the highest bidder at R21-00 a kilogram. The people are aware of the value of *Sengaparile*. Ms Hilda Motshoari said that the time is now for the project to be registered so that they obtain the necessary recognition for their part as conservers and harvesters of *Sengaparile*.

Working Conditions
There is no regulation or policy in place that directs the operations of the harvesters. Their indigenous knowledge about what they do is enough motivation for carrying out their tasks. The project is not properly monitored by the government officials from the Department of Agriculture and Conservation. The fact that they are doing a good job by harvesting *Sengaparile*

seems to be courageous enough for the Department to give them markets, which are unfortunately led by the white middleman. The harvesters have no protective clothes, no transport, no proper resting place, let alone ablution block. Harvesting *Sengaparile* is not easy. It demands energy, skills and dedication. The harvesters do the work because there is no alternative employment in the community.

Since they belong to a team they work together and encourage each other. The men are always ready to give a hand to the women who struggle with the soil. This I found a positive move. They see better results in doing that. As when I left with Ms Hilda a sack full of tubers had to fit in the boot of my car and another half was also loaded. They see collective labour as something very positive for them.

One of the ladies (Dinah) said that young people do not want to participate in the harvesting or be part of the job. Others ask questions like: how much money do you make? She said the people who are not employed and do not want to harvest will spend years in that situation, as there are no future prospects. The work they do, she said, should be seen by officials who want to buy *Sengaparile* by sending middlemen who are not prepared to pay reasonable prices.

My own opinion is that the officials should visit the harvesters during the fieldwork to see how they struggle with the reality of harvesting. They do the best out of a situation that is not covered by labour conditions. They work with no recognition in terms of labour relations. They put their life at risk and do not get the best deal. Furthermore my observation on arrival at the site was that the workers were looking at how they could survive by earnings from the project.

After the harvesting, the *Sengaparile* is chopped into small pieces. It is then laid out in the open air and hot sun to dry up. This is an effective way of drying up the medicinal plant. There is growing demand for *Sengaparile* from middlemen outside the province. The plant leaves the North-West Province without quantification, research on production, quality and quantity. Therefore the province has no record of exports based on real figures. The project is under conservation but the relevant government department does not develop the interests of the workers, their socio- economic needs are not catered for. Workers in the project are kept in high spirits by their collective understanding of knowledge based fundamentals – i.e., they have heritage resources that should provide for their livelihoods.

Discussion

From the case study above is has become clear that today there is a growing interest in natural and traditional African medicines. Powerful pharmaceutical companies are already moving in to lay claim to our natural heritage. There is an ongoing recognition and acknowledgement that traditional African medicine, unlike the analytically-based Western medicine, takes a holistic approach which addresses health, diseases, spiritual disorders, success or misfortune, which arise from the displeasure of our ancestors or the balance or imbalance of individuals and their social environment.

The ancestors revealed the natural resources of medicinal plants to traditional African health practitioners over thousands of years and taught them the ways of conserving and managing this natural heritage. Missionaries and successive colonial governments dismissed traditional African health practitioners as pagans or witches and enacted the Suppression of Witchcraft Act (Act 1959) to eradicate the practice.

The question is: Can IPR assist in developing and protecting indigenous knowledge? Demsetz, cited in Brush (1996), argues that granting property rights is a familiar method for converting public goods into private ones. Intellectual property rights do not directly convey market value to an idea or plant that is protected. Rather, they allow the market to work where otherwise it would not, by permitting a person to exclude others from using his or her ideas or plants, except under license or royalty. Perhaps this is strong motivation for South Africa to protect its IKS and bio-diversity-related resources. This, however, can be a problem (Ntsoane 2003:64), as respondents interviewed in the study expressed reservations about private companies protecting their veld products and related knowledge systems, because of the companies' interest in profit rather than in the interest of the community. They feared that they would be alienated from the sources of their being.

But if we accept that the purpose of an IPR system is to protect the rights of knowledge holders for the public good, it should be possible for all those with useful knowledge of economic or cultural value to secure protection (Dutfield 2000: 70). It is common knowledge amongst western countries, that 'without intellectual property, all ideas are public goods or common property, and no one can be excluded from using another's idea'. People in developing countries continue to use traditional medicine.

It is estimated that about eighty percent of South Africans consult traditional health practitioners, using many of the traditional medicines derived from plants. They are attracted to traditional African medicine because it is a holistic discipline involving the extensive use of indigenous herbs, combined with aspects of African spirituality.

From time immemorial traditional African medicine has been making a valuable contribution to primary health care. Its uses and experiences have been handed down orally from generation to generation. This is the greatest heritage that indigenous African resources still own despite years of colonial intrusion on African forests and sacred places. The harvesters in the case study are part of the community that for many years lived on natural resources and used medical plants for their healing and for a nutritional immune boost.

South Africa has one of the richest natural resource of medicinal plants to be found anywhere on earth. Over 30,000 species grace this vast and diverse landscape with an estimated 3,000 species of plants used as traditional medicines. The North-West province has some of the rare medicinal plants as part of its bio-diversity. Maria Ascencão reports that the Western Cape area alone rivals the tropical rain forests with over 99,000 species and has been classified as being the most diverse temperate flora on earth. In comparison, only approximately 2000 species of medical and aromatic plants are traded in Europe, including around 1300 that are native to the continent. Ethno-botanical information from traditional African health workers is validating the healing properties and nutritional value of indigenous African systems of medicine.

This discussion demonstrates that the collectors of medicinal plants make a lot of money for themselves without the benefit being shared with those communities that over the years protected the bio-diversity from extinction.

Scientists from all over the world believe that the natural heritage of Africa can supply healing via medicines and herbal know-how. A need has arisen for scientists and traditional African health practitioners to work together to validate this ancient African herbal healing. However, the playing field is not level. Traditional African health practitioners have extensive knowledge and expertise of plant species and their ecology, but have not documented this. This is a challenge for protection of both the know-how and the use of plants. The scientists who collaborate with them are given information and accumulate experience of the use of herbs, and they merely validate this information to meet modern-day health regulations. After the validation they document the information, publish books, and claim intellectual property which was imparted to traditional African health practitioners by their ancestral spirits and wisdom teachings which the scientists do not recognise. In cases where they benefit, traditional health practitioners are given a once-off payment or royalties. This contravenes the CBD which 'is rooted in the principle that benefits from using genetic resources should be shared. However, TRIPS promotes the privatization of genetic resources, not benefit sharing' (Meadley 2000).

It is generally acknowledged that ethno-botanical research and development and scientific validation of the chemistry, pharmacology and clinical evaluation of traditional African medicinal plants and the preservation of this ancient knowledge within a modern paradigm is critically important. But this operation is technically driven and it merely verifies what is already known. These technical services should oblige the scientists to pay for professional services rendered, and not to claim intellectual property rights because there is nothing they discover themselves, they merely verify and document. This is a service that the state should be providing to traditional African health practitioners at no cost and in the public interest. Perhaps IKS policy should critically look into the services that the state will have to provide in keeping up with Convention of Biological Diversity and other international agreement that positively support the developing countries. The Rio Treaty requires each member country to prevent bio-piracy and develop strategies for looking after its plant heritage and ensuring that natural resources remain the intellectual property of the individual country.

The modernisation of herbal medicines, without due regard to their underlying spirituality, not only erodes the efficacy of these herbs but also alienates the inheritance of traditional healers and vests it in pharmaceutical companies which make these medicines and foodstuffs inaccessible to their original owners.

Increasingly, South African scientists and numerous universities are conducting indigenous plant research and development, and thus pave the way forward to conserve our natural plant knowledge and resources within the South African context. These scientists and science councils use state resources to collect and document the information from indigenous communities, but they do not discover anything new themselves. Nevertheless, they acquire the intellectual property rights to these herbal medicines. There is an urgent need to protect traditional health practitioners against middlemen, local scientists and foreign pharmaceutical companies.

Western countries are aware of the uniquely diverse and abundant biological heritage and they have a huge demand for South African plants.

Challenges Facing Stakeholders in IKS

From time immemorial African people obtained divine knowledge about medicinal and nutritional plants from their guardians or ancestral spirits who also taught them special ways of relating to nature and the environment and to honour the gods for the knowledge they continuously imparted to humanity. There has always been this interdependence between traditional Africans and the plant resources and other natural products, which were harvested for medicinal and nutritional purposes.

The colonisation of Africa brought with it market forces which see profit in everything and which have no regard for the spiritual sources of indigenous African knowledge systems and the need to appropriate the guardian spirits which impart the knowledge to us.

Traditional African health practitioners have little knowledge of the market and of intellectual property rights, and they lack the knowledge to run specialised botanical businesses. Market forces have gained access to indigenous African knowledge systems and are registering patents abroad, denying Africans access to their own medicinal and nutritional plants and thus creating diseases and hunger in the land of plenty. The undermining of traditional rights of local communities to bio-diversity and hence a weakening of their capacity to conserve bio-diversity is the impact of IPR (Shiva 1997:88).

African people have lost their mineral rights to a handful of people and now they run the risk of losing the fundamental basis of their existence, which is their natural plant and cultural heritage. TRIPS has provisions that can make it illegal for farmers to replant seeds that their ancestors have used for centuries without paying royalties to patent holders (Madeley 2000:96). We therefore need to look at sustainable development that will help preserve traditional lifestyles by protecting our plant resources upon which the majority of South Africans depend for primary health care and income.

Madeley (2000: 94-5) posits that around ninety-seven percent of all the world's patents are held by companies in Western countries. These countries and their private companies should, first, recognise the national sovereign right of countries to their biological wealth. Secondly, they have to recognise the contribution of indigenous communities to knowledge about the utilisation of bio-diversity. According to Shiva (2001:122), recognition of sovereignty and indigenous knowledge creates a major shift in the political context of the ownership, use and control of genetic resources, especially in the areas of agricultural bio-diversity, including seeds and plant genetic resources.

The whole business of patents is stacked in favour of transnational corporations and against the interests of small farmers. If poverty has to be reduced to zero by 2015, the international community should change its patent rules to protect resource-poor-farmers. Although there are difficulties with IPR and TRIPs, developing countries should not be disillusioned with IPR. According to Dutfield (2000), trademarks and geographical indications may be appropriate forms of protection for some products based on indigenous knowledge, even if they cannot protect the knowledge per se. The other issue is that policy makers schooled in Western legal systems are apt to suppose that the only IPR which exists are the ones referred to in TRIPS and the WIPO-administered conventions. Dutfield (ibid) concludes that local and indigenous communities often have very complex custom-based intellectual property systems.

The struggle that harvesters experienced with middlemen and the absence of legal protection for their indigenous knowledge and natural resource shows that it is about time that policy makers and law makers look at other models other than the western IPR to protect their indigenous knowledge systems. Dutfield (ibid) observes that 'just as local communities can benefit from learning about the western IPR tradition, it is about time that lawyers, policy makers and industrial users of biological resources also learned about how traditional communities generate, use, manage and control their own knowledge'.

References

Crops and Robbers, 1999, *Biopiracy and the Patent of Staple Food Crops*, London, Action Aid, November.

Dutfield, Graham, 2000, *Intellectual Property Rights, Trade and Bio-diversity*, United Kingdom, Earthscan Publication Ltd.

Laliberte, Ron, P. Settee, J.B. Waldram, et al. eds., 2000, *Expressions in Canadian Native Studies*, Saskatchewan, University of Saskatchewan Extension Press.

Meadly, J., 2000, *Hungry for Trade*, David Philip, Cape Town.

Ntsoane, O, 2003, in *Popularisation of Science and Technology Education: Some Case Studies from Africa*, M. Savage and P. Naidoo. eds., United Kingdom, Commonwealth Secretariat.

Shiva, Vandana, 1997, *Biopiracy: The Plunder of Nature and Knowledge*, Toronto, Between the line.

Shiva, Vandana, 2001, *Protect or Plunder? Understanding Intellectual Property Rights*, Cape Town, David Philip.

Watal, Jayasheree, 2001, *Intellectual Property Rights in the WTO and Developing Countries*, Oxford, Oxford University Press.

World Intellectual Property Organisation, 2002, *Intergovernmental Committee on Intellectual Property and Genetic Resources, Traditional Knowledge and Folklore*, Third Session, Geneva, 13-21 June.

9

Protection and Promotion of Local Music: A Talent that Educates, Entertains and Binds

Wapula Nelly Raditloaneng

Introduction

Music is soothing to the heart and ministers to our emotional and spiritual needs. With modernisation, commercialisation and globalisation – issues related to copyright and laws governing private ownership, recording and registration of musical artworks have emerged.

There are three dimensions pertinent to the discourse around protecting local talent. The first dimension focuses on the ethics of protecting music and thus condoning private ownership and commercialisation. This dimension serves to foster the exploitation of musicians, as it is not in the best interest of the capitalists to fairly reward talent. The second dimension is the 'Go back to our roots' attitude through which we adopt a 'laissez-faire' attitude and do not take any legislative action to protect local music. Meanwhile music is available for use as the need arises. Third is the challenge to assess the protective laws in place and fine-tune them for proper enforcement. National and international legislation must be enacted if it is in the nation's best interest to protect local music and thereby promote equality in recognising various talents. Music does not only meet social needs but quite a number of artists play music as a source of livelihood. As individuals, and collectively, people find refuge in music. Therefore, the need to protect local music as a treasured talent is overdue.

A Brief History and Context of Music in Botswana

Very little is written about the history of musical cultures in Botswana (Norborg 1987). What is known is that Batswana are part of the Bantu language-speakers in Southern Africa. Within Botswana itself there lived the San, Bakgalagadi, and of course the rest of the Tswana speaking groups in the eighteenth century. All these groups had their own musical instruments and traditional songs.

Since 1966 when Botswana gained political independence from Britain, a number of developments have occurred not just in music but other service sectors. Western instruments have been officially acquired for example by the Botswana Defence Force and Botswana Police bands. Botswana is largely dependent on recording studios and companies in South Africa. Since the early 1990s, as if Batswana had just only become aware of their talent, more and more of them have made a conscious decision to earn a living out of music. A significant number of Batswana singers have formed music troupes and recorded musical albums on disc and audio-cassettes.

Sponsorship is very limited. The National Cultural Council within the Ministry of Labour and Home Affairs promotes local culture by allocating government money to selected groups. However, the amounts awarded to the groups are very limited and therefore inadequate to effectively promote music as a source of living for local musicians. On a few occasions, music festivals are held to promote non- profit making organisations.

The Role of Music in Educating, Entertaining, Binding and Storage of Information

Education

My definition of education, which is also experiential, is that it is a process of acquiring knowledge, skills, attitudes and practices beyond the four walls of the classroom. Education comes within a particular discourse. There are distinct socio- economic classes that permeate the local music industry in Botswana. Music therefore has an educational, class and a gender character. It serves to increase people's skills and employability. Education is a component of lifelong learning.

Local music serves to provide a unique resource for lifelong learning and active citizenship that can be used to discuss issues of common interests and significance. For instance, music can be used to educates on the need to fight the scourge of HIV/AIDS, promotes productivity, nationhood, and cultural beliefs, and challenges traditional stereotypes. Music itself is very educative in terms of instilling culturally acceptable behaviour. The significant role of music echoes my beliefs in social change that takes place in the realm of the mind and observable human behaviour. For instance, if people pay attention and meditate on the messages that promote the educative role of music, we may be compelled to rethink our actions and transform the way we behave by unlearning, and adopting socially acceptable behaviour.

The great talents of musicians raise questions like: What counts as experience and whose experience counts most? What is the educational background or qualification of the musicians in relation to other people with related talents? If people treasure music as both an individual and a social asset, then the experiences of local musicians count as experiences worthy of recognition and reward like other forms of human creation. Education and certification do not always match performance. While education embraces some form of organised or unorganised instruction by teachers of children and facilitators in adult education, lifelong learning is everybody's business. It does not require an instructor, a budget, infrastructure, or any equipment. Education is therefore a supreme and authentic member of the household while lifelong learning, including learning through music, is the 'poor cousin' as Newman (1994) contends. However, the concepts of learning itself and useful knowledge are usually defined by dominant discourses from the west, so that marginality and disadvantage are socially constructed to infringe on the rights of local musicians in Botswana and other Third World countries. Lifelong learning is therefore embedded in social relationships.

Entertainment

Music is entertainment at various cultural and political occasions. Cultural gatherings (*manyalo, molaletsa, letsema, kgotla, mephato*), are usually graced with well-known songs. Mass choirs, drama, dance troupes, marimba groups, and other forms of entertainment usually characterise weddings, graduation ceremonies and others. A wedding not graced with music is usually boring. The pleasure of listening to good music is a many-sided affair. The voice, rhythm, and tune combine to sooth those who need it. Music is a kind of amusement even for children too (Blacking, 1967).

Music as a Binder

Music is a binding force that seals the cultural identity of Batswana as a nation and its connection to the African continent. As in other Third World countries, Botswana culture continues to suffer oppression from the former colonisers and other Batswana who discount everything local as primitive and not worthwhile. Songs that culturally bind include pieces like our national anthem of the Republic of Botswana, '*Fatshe leno la rona. Ke mpho ya Modimo. Ke boswa jwa bo rraetsho. A le nne ka kagiso*' (This is our land. It is God's gift to us. It is our inheritance. Let there be peace'). Others include '*Ditlhopho di tsile*' (It is election time). These songs urge Batswana to register for parliamentary elections so that they can go to the polls in great numbers at election time. Music thus helps to sensitise, remind, and bind Batswana around common family, community themes, and national values.

Protest songs against apartheid in South Africa, racism in Namibia, AIDS/ HIV in Botswana and Uganda, provide a particular kind of education, solidarity, hope, learning and support for popular struggles for human rights and democracy. Music illuminates political struggles and can help build solidarity and patriotism within and between countries and different cultures. Similarly, Botswana as a nation supported South African refugees who came to Botswana to seek refuge. Batswana learned musical items composed in different languages including Zulu and Xhosa. These are songs of hope in which refugees envisioned a free South Africa, Angola and Mozambique.

Another regionally popular slogan is '*Aluta continua*' (The struggle continues). The slogan is based on hopes and a positive profession that life is about struggles and challenges everyone must willingly face and fight winning battles. Although Batswana, (sandwiched between different factions of warring countries), as a nation received their independence on a silver platter, they emotionally, materially and verbally support neighbouring countries in their struggle for political independence. Determination to make the world a better place is a key feature expressed in local, national and international music.

Music and the Cultural Storage of Information

Music is an important store of information for the storage and transmission of historical information and facts from one generation to another. Botswana has a national television station and several national radio stations that contribute to promoting local talent. However, questions that arise are: What kind of musical programmes does Botswana Television and Radio promote? Both BTV and radio broadcasters use local music without paying any fees and royalties to the artists. Botswana still has a long way to go before proudly claiming patriotism and protection of local talent. Local music is under siege by the global world that comprises individual researchers, government officials, and international communities. With this gloomy picture, what hope is left for local musicians? It is important to look again at local music and correct wrongs in failing to assure quality and promote and protect local musicians.

Promoting and Protecting Local Talent

As mentioned earlier, music is an intrinsic ingredient of lifelong learning. It is not surprising that its survival is not effectively promoted and protected. Like non-formal, informal and incidental learning, music is marginal and not treated as mainstream. Past records of tertiary institutions indicate that music educators are under-represented in the education sector.

There are challenges that arise with policies that promote culture, tradition, heritage and identity.

The Rights of Musicians

According to the Southern African Music Rights Organization (SAMRO), (2001), in musical work, there are three main categories of rights: Graphic rights, mechanical rights, and performing rights. Graphic rights deal with the right to print music. Mechanical rights have to do with recording. Performing rights are the right to control the performance of music in public, including the right to broadcast. SAMRO further argues that 'Just as the labourer is worthy of his hire, so is the creator entitled to an equitable remuneration for the use of his work by others' (Pamphlet 1). In other African countries including Kenya, Uganda and South Africa, National Music Councils exist to protect local musicians (Opondo, 2000, p. 18). Similarly, the government of Botswana needs to enact and enforce legislation to protect local musicians.

According to Frith, (cited by Opondo, 2000): 'Music is one of the most universal human experiences. Every culture experiences music in some form... Music educators must be willing to lead' (p.1). Frith further argues that national and international legislation is important to enact for protection of indigenous musicians.

The Copyright and Neighbouring Rights Act

Two issues in particular have dominated recent music industry attempts to change copyright laws: home taping and digital sampling. The record industry mounts blank tapes and therefore promotes home taping that amounts to 'theft' and 'murder' of the music industry. Home tapers are accused of taking pleasure from an artist's work without payment. Home tapers steal the author's creativity. In developed countries (Austria, France, Germany) a levy on blank audio and video cassettes has been placed with success, though in some cases even the levy has failed to deter violation of copyright laws.

Copyright as a human right is acquired upon creation. Local musicians, however, must price their product. Copyright is very important to give the exclusive right of use and disposal. Botswana, like other Southern African countries, has a Copyright Act. Unfortunately, pending the implementation regulations, the Act is not yet in force.

Challenges in Protecting Local Music

According to Anyindoho and Tsikata (1998), protecting local musicians poses several challenges:

Firstly, there is a problem of identification of oral works for copyright: 'English law... considers that there can be no copyright unless the work has been written down, recorded or otherwise reduced to material form (p.146). The problem of oral works affects African music and dance. Secondly, music falls within folklore in the African context. The definition of the scope of folklore is problematic in Africa. It is also problematic to extend copyright to living folklore.

Thirdly, while African countries have been colonised and therefore dance to the tune of the former colonisers, there is a problem of applying European musical ideology to the African musical realm. African music uses multiple rhythms. It is problematic to judge the worth of each rhythm by foreign standards.

Fourthly, ethnic hegemony is a factor in the promotion or a hindrance to traditional music. Language diversity in Botswana means that while rhythms may be similar, it may not be possible to promote the music of minority ethnic groups. Within the context of their geographical location, minority ethnic groups can promote their own music. Beyond their geographical location, traditional music from the dominant ethnic groups predominates. While this is a unifying factor suggestive of the need to foster unity, it may not go down well with people of minority ethnic groups. Ethnicity, effective communication, and language barriers work to disadvantage some societal groups and disadvantage others. This may promote or hinder music depending on the power of the different stakeholders in music.

Lastly, recording well-known traditional music by Botswana artists will pose several questions for the implementation of copyright legislation. The major question would be: Who is eligible to record well known traditional music? How many such people would be allowed to record and who would be the recipient of royalties? Copyright legislation may be enforced to limit the recording of such music to one person. Who would be that one person and why would they be given the right to record well-known traditional music?

Maybe like other trade union movements, local musicians should form unions for bargaining power and dialogue on problems of representation in international forums. Globalisation of music is an irreversible phenomenon and there is no need to sweep and hide dust under the carpet and claim it is not-existent.

Implications for Adult Life-long Learning

Adult Education has a strong legacy of advocacy for the plight of socially disadvantaged groups. Promotion and protection of the local music industry is therefore part of the business of adult educators globally.

To the literates, the music industry involves an understanding of ways in which power is distributed unequally within the social structure so that practices of some are marginalised while others are privileged. Learning is for individual and social change. It provides an opportunity for people to make sense of the world and act upon it through music. To the non- literate, the desire to learn may not be very high. The non-literates may not be in a position to know and filter information like the literates. The non-literates may be so 'economically asleep' that they may not be in a position to know how to and discern the economic benefits of music because of lack of knowledge. Adult educators must be sensitive to learning through music as it has a class, a gender, a political character and breeds diverse emotions.

Music is a great promoter of lifelong learning. Adult lifelong learners must learn to focus on the existential meanings of music rather than get carried away with the rhythm. Facilitators must be sensitive to the meanings that people make of music.

Adult Educators must protect and promote training in music education since people can learn from music. Adult educators must be aggressive to promote, teach, and provide opportunities for lifelong learning. They must prove that learning goes beyond the four walls of the classroom.

Conclusions

From the discussion above, it is unquestionable that the use of music has grown and continues to do so in importance. Music has to be moved into the mainstream and not peripheral to other forms of education. Musicians are talented and vested with indispensable knowledge that is relevant to sensitising the nation on diverse issues of common cultural interest.

Despite the many constraints that local musicians face, there seems to be an understanding and a desire to continue with the talent. It is therefore very important that local musicians are protected from physical and social harm. Of great significance is the need to at least reward talent regardless of the academic background and officially recognised credentials of musicians. A Copyright Association may be a spokesperson for the talented beneficiaries of music. As a compassionate and caring society, Botswana has to culturally unlearn the marginalisation and exploitation of talents and learn to recognise and reward at the highest possible political level. This paper serves as a wake up call to deconstruct the myths and construct knowledge on how to promote and protect local music - a talent that educates, entertains, binds and serves as a national memory for storage of information.

References

Anyindoho, K., and Tsikata, F., 1988, *Copyright and Oral Literature*, Music Education Course Packet.

Battish, F.L., 1999, *Teaching Music - the Leadership Component*, Grand Masters Series, Music Education Journal.

Blacking, J., 1967, *Venda Children's Song: A Study in Ethno-musicological Analysis*, Chicago, The University of Chicago Press.

Hoffer, C.R., 1993, *Introduction to Music Education*, Belmont, California, Wadsworth Publishing Company.

Kamien, R., 1996, *Music – An Appreciation*, Sixth Edition, New York, McGraw-Hill Companies, Inc.

Newman, M., 1994, *Defining the Enemy: Adult Education in Social Action*, Sydney, Stewart Victor Publishing.

Norborg, A., 1987, *A Handbook of Musical and other Sound-Producing Instruments from Namibia and Botswana*, Musikmuseets Skifter 13, Stockholm, Blomsbokryckeri AB, Lund.

Opondo, P.A., 2000, 'Cultural Policies in Kenya', *Arts Education Policy Review Symposium*, Vol. 101 (5).

Southern African Music Rights Organisation, 2001, *Pamphlet1*, Johannesburg, SAMRO.

Index

www.ingramcontent.com/pod-product-compliance
Lightning Source LLC
Chambersburg PA
CBHW021832020426
42334CB00014B/598